DISCARD

THE EDISON SCHOOLS

CORPORATE
SCHOOLING
AND THE
ASSAULT
ON PUBLIC
EDUCATION

KENNETH J. SALTMAN

ROUTLEDGE
NEW YORK AND LONDON

Published in 2005 by
Routledge
270 Madison Avenue
New York, NY 10016
www.routledge-ny.com

Published in Great Britain by
Routledge
2 Park Square
Milton Park, Abingdon
Oxon OX14 4RN U.K.
www.routledge.co.uk

10 9 8 7 6 5 4 3 2 1

Library of Congress Cataloging-in-Publication Data for this book is available
from the Library of Congress

ISBN 0-415-94841-X
ISBN 0-415-95046-5 (pbk.)

Library of Congress Cataloging-in-Publication Data

Saltman, Kenneth J., 1969-
    The Edison Schools : corporate schooling and the assault on public education /
Kenneth J. Saltman.
        p. cm. -- (Positions : education, politics, and culture)
    Includes bibliographical references and index.
    ISBN 0-415-94841-X (hardback : alk. paper) -- ISBN 0-415-95046-5
    (pbk.: alk. paper)
    1. Privatization in education--United States--Case studies. 2. Business
    education--United States--Case studies. 3. EdisonSchools Inc.--Case studies.
    I. Title. II. Series: Positions
    (Routledge (Firm))
LB2806.36.S26 2005

                                                                2004018898

Series Editors' Introduction

Positions is a series interrogating the intersections of education, politics, and culture. Books in the series are short, polemical, and accessibly written, merging rigorous scholarship with politically engaged criticism. They focus on both pressing contemporary topics and historical issues that continue to define and inform the relationship between education and society.

"Positions" as a term refers to the obvious position that authors in the series take, but it might also refer to the "war of position" described by Italian cultural theorist Antonio Gramsci, who emphasized the centrality of political struggles over meanings, language, and ideas to the battle for civil society. We believe that these struggles over meanings, language, and ideas are crucial for the making of a more just social order in which political, cultural, and economic power is democratically controlled. We believe, as Paulo Freire emphasized, that there is no way not to take a position.

The current volume in the series, *The Edison Schools: Corporate Schooling and the Assault on Public Education*, takes the position that the largest corporation involved in public school privatization threatens to undermine not only public schooling but ultimately the American public itself. Most writing on Edison and the EMO (Educational Management Organization) has focused on the success or failure of Edison as a business and on the efficiency or inefficiency of Edison as a "deliverer" of educational services. *The Edison Schools* extensively covers these debates but goes much further by illustrating that what is really at stake in the story of Edison is the way corporate schooling stands starkly against the progressive promises of schooling for a more democratic society. *The Edison Schools* takes a position against public school privatization and for strengthening public schooling, using the bellwether of the privatization debates as example. It highlights the ways that public school privatization initiatives threaten teaching as a profession, undermine the stability of schools and teacher work, cost more, and target those students and schools most in need of strengthened public provision. In keeping with the aims of the series, *The Edison Schools* reframes the very public school privatization debates by suggesting that the key questions are not exclusively the ones that corporate America would have us believe—those of cost and test score efficiency—but rather crucial matters of social vision, public priority, and collective values.

KENNETH J. SALTMAN
ASSISTANT PROFESSOR, SOCIAL AND CULTURAL STUDIES IN EDUCATION
DEPAUL UNIVERSITY

RON SCAPP
ASSOCIATE PROFESSOR OF EDUCATION AND PHILOSOPHY
DIRECTOR OF THE MASTER'S PROGRAM IN URBAN AND
MULTICULTURAL EDUCATION
THE COLLEGE OF MOUNT ST. VINCENT

ACKNOWLEDGMENTS

I am extremely grateful to Robin Truth Goodman for repeatedly reading drafts, editing, discussing ideas, and making helpful suggestions on the manuscript. I thank Routledge Education Editor Catherine Bernard for her tremendous support and very thoughtful close editing on this project. Without her suggestions this would be a very different book. A number of people generously shared with me published information on Edison. These include especially Peter Wissoker, Caroline Grannan, Rico Gutstein, Erik Badger, Emily Vasilion, Alex Molnar, and Sheila Macrine, as well as Andrew and Michelle Decker and Charles and Carla Szybist. As well, several people generously shared with me firsthand accounts of their experiences with Edison. I am very grateful to Caroline Grannan, Marc Bainbridge, Elaine Simon, and Sukey Blanc. A number of people were crucially helpful in discussing the issues, especially Pauline Lipman, Enora Brown, Ros Mickelson, and Kathy Szybist. A number of friends suffered early drafts or made important comments and suggestions for significant changes, especially Henry Giroux, Pepi Leistyna, Ron Scapp, Stephen Haymes, and Pauline Lipman. I also thank Donaldo Macedo, Peter McLaren, Susan Giroux, David Gabbard, Kevin Bunka and Wayne Ross for their continued support, exchange, and inspiration.

INTRODUCTION

Pledging Allegiance to the Corporation

A mild breeze blows the steam from the coffee in the paper cup I am holding. Sun is shining, sky is blue with perfect clouds, and if the parking brake holds on the borrowed compact car parked on a 40-degree incline in the Mission District, then this tour of San Francisco's only Edison school should be fine. I am standing in the courtyard doorway of Edison Charter Academy and it is about quarter to eight in the morning in the autumn of 2003. The mostly Mexican American kids are lining up in neat columns shouldering backpacks before a tall flagpole, and a dapper white man in a suit stands beside it.

As the students recite the pledge before the flag, I recall my own public school education, the morning pledge. I quickly realize it is not the pledge of allegiance to the flag of the United States of America that the students are repeating. I strain to make out the chorused words as they overlap, words carried across the asphalt schoolyard to my ears:

> As a student at
> Edison Charter Academy
> I pledge to respect myself
> Respect my teachers
> Respect my fellow students
> And respect my building
> I will do nothing to keep the teacher from
> Teaching and anyone, myself included from, learning.

These students are attending a school paid for by public resources. They are not expected to pledge their allegiance to the nation or its flag. Rather, they are lined up in front of the nation's flag as they recite this pledge to themselves and to the Edison Schools corporation, the nation's largest for-profit education company.[1]

In 2003, Edison Schools, the largest educational management organization, or EMO, in the nation, claimed to be running schools for 132,000 U.S. public school students in 20 states and, as of the 2001–2002 school year, it ran 136 public schools in 23 states. It was founded in 1992 as, The Edison Project, by former *Esquire* magazine publisher and Channel One entrepreneur, Chris Whittle. EMOs like Edison are different from private schools. Private schools collect tuition from parents or guardians for private educational services. EMOs like Edison seek contracts with school districts or states to run public schools for profit. These companies aim to use tax money to run public schools and extract profits for investors from the money that would otherwise go to pay for smaller class sizes, more books and other supplies, and higher teacher salaries. There is something quite new, quite radical, and possibly quite ominous happening in the yard at Edison Charter Academy. Public school students are being instructed in pledging themselves to the corporation.

Part of why it matters to tell this story is that Edison has been not just one experiment in public school privatization but the experiment in corporations taking over public schools to run them for profit. Of 47 EMOs profiled in 2003 by the Commercialism in Education Research Unit at Arizona State University, Edison was by far the largest, in charge of more than a quarter of the 417 schools run by these EMOs in 24 states.[2] Despite a number of failed and largely forgotten experiments with privatization in the 1970s, 1980s, and 1990s, Edison has appeared in the press as the bellwether of the school privatization movement. Edison's successes have been interpreted by journalists and education experts as indication that the privatization movement will expand. Its failures have been hailed as proof that privatization of schools cannot work.

The story of Edison has been so volatile and unpredictable that simply writing about it has been particularly difficult. As I finished the first draft of the manuscript, Edison was suffering a drastic loss in the value of its stock, it was embroiled in controversy over test scores, it was desperately seeking operating cash from investors, it was being protested in the streets, and it was on the verge of taking over 60 of the schools in the Philadelphia School District. Getting the Philadelphia schools would have likely inspired investor confidence in Edison and would have possibly fueled the company's expansion. Before the next round of revisions on my manuscript, Edison went from appearing on the verge of financial collapse,[3] with a radically dwindled stock price and the loss of several contracts with schools, to an announcement by founder and company head Chris Whittle that for the first time profitability was on the way. Before the next round of revisions, news came that the shares of the publicly traded company would be bought back by investors. The volatility of the company has been highlighted by Edison's critics as symptomatic of a major problem with businesses running schools. If accountability is maintained by the looming threat of companies like Edison going out of business, then what happens to school kids when the company running their school goes under? What is at stake in the story of Edison is more than a topsy-turvy story of a struggling company with a colorful leader at the helm. What is at stake is a broad program of transforming public goods and services into investment opportunities for the wealthiest citizens.

In the last two decades corporations have become increasingly interested in education. Although this interest is frequently dressed up in the language of excellence, success, achievement, and individual self-actualization, there are two principal reasons that corporations care about schooling. These reasons have more to do with the bottom line than with individual virtues or social uplift. The first reason has to do with corporations being able to profit financially from schools. By the late 1990s a number of companies were attempting to build education conglomerates. Conservative think tanks, investment banks, and business magazines were increasingly discussing the profit potential of investing in schooling, and they were describing the public school system as a potential $600 billion investment opportunity, comparing it to both the health care industry and the defense sector.

Corporate profit in public schooling can take the form of advertising in schools, running schools for a profit, or less directly controlling the curriculum to ensure that schools teach what is useful for corporations, thereby saving companies worker training costs or even advertising costs. Another indirect yet extremely important role of schools for the corporate sector involves producing a disciplined workforce willing to submit to wage labor and the organization of time and work by others in positions of authority. Following the rules of the teacher readies the kids to submit to the boss. Although most people need to learn to submit to the authority of others at certain times, the pertinent question is whether or not schools should be principally involved in making disciplined workers and consumers or, rather, in educating citizens for civic engagement — that is, in educating citizens to understand the world and to change it with others so that it is more just, equal, democratic, and free.

Corporations and their leaders are also concerned with preventing efforts to improve public education by redistributing educational resources in ways that are most equitable or by restructuring the educational funding system. Although nearly always transformed by advocates of privatization into a matter of the most effective school reform methods, the argument against spending more to improve all public schools or against taking money from rich locales to improve poor locales coincides with the economic interests of those at the top of the economy who stand to benefit from current funding arrangements. In other words, those who own and work for corporations tend not to want the educational privileges they receive in the form of excellent public schools to be diminished in order to improve the schools of poor and working-class citizens.

For the most part, the public schools that Edison has been given to run are in working class and poor communities. Most students at Edison schools are African American or Latino.[4] Edison does not run any schools in communities that could be characterized as economically privileged. One reason for this has to do with the way public schooling is funded in the United States. Because public schools are funded mostly by local property taxes, wealthier communities can spend more for school buildings, teaching supplies, administration, extracurricular programs, and technology. They can also pay higher salaries and attract the teachers and administrators that they want. U.S. public schools in economically privileged communities are some of the highest-performing and best schools in the world by conventional standards.

Despite these facts, tremendous effort and resources are invested by corporations and think tanks in arguing that resources do not really matter, that what really matters is educational methods. Another fallacy with the argument that money does not matter appears in the willingness of many advocates of privatization to see federal money going to states and corporations that embrace the methodological reforms that they tend to agree with. The Bush Administration's No Child Left Behind plan emphasizes heavy testing and phonics-based reading instruction typifying this refusal to fund public schools without attaching strings. No Child Left Behind will guarantee that test-publishing and textbook-publishing companies benefit massively from the reform. As a number of chapters detail, Edison has longstanding ties to the Bush Administrations and family.

The second reason corporations and their leaders care about schools is ideological. In the view of corporations, the public sector is bureaucratic, inefficient, and incompetent while the private sector is responsible for (nearly) all that is good in the world. This view of the world coincides with the financial profit of corporations and the shifting of public resources to the private sector where profit can be extracted for wealthy individuals. This is not a conspiracy of overfed cigar-puffing men in three-piece suits sitting in smoke-filled backrooms wringing their hands with delight as they scheme to privatize public schooling. Corporations and private interests exist to make profit. They seek to do so any way they can. Public institutions ideally exist to serve the public interest rather than for the accumulation of profit. Part of what is at stake in the Edison story and in the trend of privatization more generally is the ways that public goals, aspirations, and ways of describing the world have been largely replaced by private goals, aspirations, and ways of describing the world. As the chapters in this book illustrate, this cultural shift away from thinking and talking about the public interest and toward a business vision for the future has been the result of a number of factors, including the consolidation of mass media such that a handful of large, profit-motivated media corporations largely frame public issues in the corporate interest. Popular press coverage of Edison exemplifies this tendency. In more than a thousand articles written in the popular press about Edison, the vast majority focus on its success or failure as a business and whether or not its test performance indicates that success as a business.[5] Precious little of the press coverage explores in depth the implications for a democratic society of for-profit businesses running public schools. As well, right-wing think tanks such as the Heritage Foundation, Hoover Institution, American Enterprise Institute, Cato Institute, Hudson Institute, Manhattan Institute, and the Scaife Foundation, not to mention business organizations such as the Business Roundtable, have succeeded in steering public policy and national debate by placing spokespeople in mass media and government to assure a business-oriented perspective when it comes to making decisions about the future of public priorities such as schooling, health care, social security, and the environment. In 2002, 47 percent of print and broadcast citations of think tanks were "conservative," 41 percent were "centrist," and 12 percent were "progressive."[6] To put some perspective on these figures and classifications, the most-cited think tank was the "centrist" Brookings Institution (4,308 citations), which has largely championed educational privatization and counts Edison's Chief Education Officer John Chubb as among its fellows. The conservative triumphs in mass media on the subject of educational privatization need to be understood in relation to corporate ownership of media, advertiser influence in media, and the consequent narrow range of debate. For-profit institutions tend not to publicize ideas and perspectives counter to the financial and ideological interests of their owners.[7] Like mass media, schools are knowledge-making institutions central to the dissemination of ideas, information, perspectives, and frameworks for understanding, interpreting, and acting.

Despite being regularly maligned in the press, U.S. public schools, when compared with public schools in other industrialized nations, fare well. Comparisons between U.S. public schools and the schools of other industrialized nations reveal U.S. students to be comparably educated to students of other industrialized nations. In 2000, "No difference was detected between the mean scores of U.S. 15-year-olds on the Program for International Student Assessment (PISA) reading literacy scale (504) and the mean scores of 15-year-olds in France, Italy, Germany, Japan, and the United Kingdom."[8] The same year mathematics and science literacy scores published by the OECD (Organization for Economic Cooperation and Development) revealed that the United States was just below the mean for member states of the OECD, scoring 493 in mathematics and 499 in science with an average OECD score of 500. The United States outscored Germany, Italy, Spain, and Portugal, among other nations, but was outscored by Japan, the United Kingdom, and Canada, among others. A number of countries including Switzerland and Norway had scores in math and science that were extremely close to the U.S. scores. Part of what this tells us is that the frequently heard hysteria about U.S. public schools "failing" (another business term) is inconsistent with the facts. It is true that some U.S. public schools are failing. However, it is important to recognize that there is a pattern of failure that thoroughly coincides with public investment and commitment. Moreover, the picture changes when one considers some of the ways that the United States is distinguished from most other OECD countries: (1) the U.S. suffers the greatest disparity in wealth and income in the industrialized world and has by far the highest rates of child poverty among industrialized countries; (2) the U.S. disproportionately funds primary and secondary education with local taxes rather than through federal distribution; (3) the U.S. puts less money relative to GDP (gross domestic product) into its education system than all large industrialized countries except the United Kingdom, which puts in the same percentage.[9] These facts suggest that the relative parity of the U.S. achievement numbers with other industrialized nations is coming *despite* distinct disadvantages suffered by many students at the bottom of the economic spectrum. Put another way, the spectacular successes of U.S. public schooling are coming at the upper end of the economy. U.S. public schools are doing a great job of educating the more privileged segments of the population.

It is a different story for public schools in communities that have suffered economic devastation, job losses, the flight of businesses to cheaper production zones, and the replacement of unionized industrial work with automation, communities burdened by not only crushing poverty but also all the social side effects of it, such as crime, violence, substance abuse, and the psychological side effects, such as feelings of hopelessness, despair, and depression not to mention displaced rage vented against women and other racial and ethnic groups.[10] Public schools in communities subject to disinvestments both suffer from a lack of educational resources and are beset by all of the problems that accompany poverty such as when parental support for students is compromised by the need for parents to work long hours at low wages or regularly move to find work. The obstacles faced by students in poor communities and schools require greater investments in those schools than in wealthy schools. An important question to ask of Edison and other EMOs is whether they achieve this. Do they afford the same opportunities to the poor students that they target as the rich students that they do not? Another, perhaps more important question to ask is whether school reform alone can address such intertwined problems as poverty, unemployment, and educational opportunity.

Public schools play a unique role in a democratic society as a place for the public debate and deliberation over social values and priorities. It is difficult for most Americans to go through a day without being bombarded by advertisements or to engage in a conversation in which the perspectives of the business sector do not dominate. Hyper-individualism, values of acquisitiveness, and status-oriented thought have only intensified in popular culture and mass media since the Reagan revolution while citizens are more than ever before being educated by profit-driven media technologies including the Internet and the expansion of cable TV. Public schools stand as one of the few places left where citizens can learn about and talk about noncommercial social and individual values and imagine hopeful futures of democratic participation in which individual and cooperative opportunities can be realized and human suffering, poverty, and discrimination can be overcome through collective public action.

Privatization of public schools takes the form of performance contracting, voucher schemes, for-profit charter schools, as well as school commercialism initiatives such as fast food and soft drink companies infiltrating public school space with advertisements from textbook content to scoreboards to the sides of buses. As the first chapter illustrates, Edison founder and CEO H. Chris Whittle has been at the forefront of multiple projects to privatize public schools. Most notably, he created Channel One, a classroom television news program with advertising. If corporations have succeeded in capturing kids for advertising in public schools, they have also succeeded in remaking the culture of schooling on the corporate model. Standardizing curriculum, the emphasis on standardized tests, and performance-based assessment are symptomatic of the near stranglehold that business ways of thinking and describing education now have on the culture of public schooling. These initiatives have been not only a boon for for-profit testing and publishing companies like ETS, Scholastic, Pearson NCS, and McGraw-Hill, but they are also ideologically effective at treating knowledge as a commodity to be consumed by students and treating knowledge as principally something to be ultimately cashed in for jobs. Heavy testing and teaching to the test, scripted lessons, pre-fab curriculum — this kind of privatization runs counter to the goals of developing in students the capacities to learn to ask critical questions, raise public concerns, engage in democratic dialogue about knowledge, about its making and circulation, and how it relates to life in a democratic society. Nearly all of the debate and writing about Edison has focused on the efficiency or inefficiency of the Edison model at delivering educational services. I take a very different direction in this book and ask larger questions about Edison in relation to the role and function of public schools in a democratic society.

Although Edison does not promise to solve the problems of poverty and unemployment that plague some communities, it does promise to offer something close: educational opportunities for students who may be able to cash in their knowledge for good jobs. For proponents of Edison Schools, Edison promises nothing less than the American dream. In fact, for supporters such as academic John Chubb, who is both a free market ideologue and an investor and Chief Educational Officer in Edison, EMOs such as Edison can bring the virtues of the private sector to the inefficient bureaucracy that they see as characterizing public schooling. Chubb, EMO entrepreneurs such as Whittle, the business press, Wall Street, as well as some unlikely allies who live in communities with dilapidated public schools, have long wanted to give the market a chance. And they claim that they have evidence proving the success and superiority of the Edison model.

For opponents of Edison Schools and other EMOs, including parents, students, teachers' unions, labor unions, and other supporters of public education, the problems of public schools cannot be reduced to alleged bureaucratic inefficiency. Strengthen public education, they say, by investing in it the same way as in the schools that appear to be most successful. According to opponents, several facts raise questions about Edison's declared idealistic intentions: if Edison believes that its management is so superior to that of the public, then why does it not try to manage the schools of wealthy communities? After all, if Edison can more efficiently manage schools than the public sector can, why do privileged communities have no interest in Edison? Could Edison not do even more good with the higher resources of wealthy communities? Put another way, would the Edison schools even exist if poor public schools and their surrounding communities were invested in the way wealthy schools are?

Critics also challenge Edison's claims of superior performance, suggesting flawed and contrived studies and real results that are mediocre and mixed (see Chapter Two). They point out that Edison uses marketing tactics and public relations campaigns to create a false spectacle of parental satisfaction in Edison schools[11] and to paint an ugly, false, and misleading portrait of public schools. Opponents suggest a very different history of the Edison schools in communities than the one painted by the corporation. Edison has been charged with excluding students from its measurements of its own success; it has also been accused of dropping from schools students with learning disabilities, special needs students, and others in need of special attention.[12] It is accused of racism for targeting minority schools for takeover, of dropping nonwhite students from score reporting, of dropping nonwhite students from schools in hopes of elevating test scores, and dropping "problem" nonwhite schools from its lineup in order, again, to show good numbers to investors and potential future clients (see Chapter Three).[13]

In addition to being a limited history of the largest educational "privatizer," this book is also a guide that aims to offer a concise yet information-rich look at the performance and history of one EMO so that if Chris Whittle or another public school privatizer shows up in your community, or in one nearby, you have enough information and history to engage in public debate about the implications for the community. This book also strives to take the debate over public school performance and efficacy to a slightly higher level by raising some broader considerations about the implications for citizens of the changing value of the public sector, the rise of the EMO as a form of privatization that is a national and even global movement, and finally the role that public schooling plays in a vibrant democracy. Before getting into these broader issues, however, we need to understand: What are the goals of Edison?

GOALS OF EDISON SCHOOLS?

Edison opened its first schools in the 1995–1996 school year with three explicit goals: (1) offer quality educational services; (2) operate schools for less money; and (3) provide more services than traditional public schools.[14]

Proponents of Edison Schools and other EMOs are true believers that the private sector can offer underfunded public schools that largely serve poor and nonwhite communities a better education than they currently receive. The fourth goal of Edison (which is harder to find on their Web site) is by far the most important because the continued existence of the company depends on it and because it is driving the company's founders and the investors who have been financing what has been to date a money-losing enterprise. This goal is to make money.

Edison's goal is to profit financially *while at the same time* satisfying parents, students, teachers, administrators, school boards, and the public that it is doing a better job than the public schools. If this sounds difficult, that is because it is. In fact, not only has this yet to be achieved, but high-profile prior attempts have ended in disaster, including the notorious case of Education Alternatives Incorporated (EAI) that briefly took over the Hartford, Connecticut public schools in 1996.[15] The inability of companies in the 1970s and 1980s to profit or stay in business demonstrated the many difficulties with performance contracting. What is different today is that Edison Schools only runs about half of its schools through performance contracting, that is, through direct partnership with the public schools themselves. The other Edison schools are run as charter schools.

Charter schools are publicly funded through tax dollars. Yet these schools operate under management contracts with school districts and charter school boards. Not all charter schools are for profit, although all Edison charter schools are for profit. Generally, charter schools have a higher degree of autonomy than partnerships operating under performance contracting. The difference between charter schools and traditional public schools lies in the extent of public oversight and public involvement in management decisions and budget allocations. The Commercialism in Education Research Unit has found that more than three-quarters of schools being opened for profit by EMOs are charter schools, suggesting that the charter school movement needs to be understood as principally functioning to facilitate public school privatization.[16] Frequently, charter schools control nearly every aspect of the school from the management of the physical site to the curriculum design to the hiring and firing of teachers, administrators, and staff. This level of control is key to the possibility of an EMO such as Edison turning a profit or going broke and closing. In order for corporations to provide investors with profits and to provide students and communities with services that are comparable to public schools, they need to cut costs.

There are only a few ways for an EMO to save money and potentially become profitable: (1) decrease local administration and centralize administration — run enough schools with centralized administration so that the per student costs are less; (2) pay teachers less and avoid teachers' unions that insist on minimum salaries and regulations on workloads; (3) pay janitorial, food service, and other staff less — typically by contracting out these services to non-unionized companies (as in most businesses, the largest cost cutting comes from decreasing labor costs); (4) to a lesser extent than items 1 through 3, standardize curriculum and control the ownership and distribution of school materials and resources. Economies of scale are of central importance to the possibility of profit here because the bigger Edison grows, the more computers, books, and chalk it orders and the cheaper it becomes to do so.

Walking through an Edison school, one is struck by how similar it looks to any other public or even private school. Initially, however, Edison schools were not supposed to look like other schools. Chris Whittle envisioned what he called "The New American School" initially hoping to compete with public schools by opening private academies that would offer more and better services than public schools. When this did not appear feasible, Edison shifted tack and sought to run public schools for profit. Edison sought to distinguish the school model in a number of ways. This mattered not only for whether or not the model would be successful in educating students, but also for appearing to investors as attractively innovative and hence worthy of startup and expansion capital.

One of the most innovative ideas was an emphasis on student and family use of technology. All students would receive a laptop computer that they could take home and use for homework. Edison emphasized a longer school day. Character education would be central to the model. Every Edison student would become bilingual through dual language instruction. Edison would use computers to track student achievement and process achievement data from headquarters in New York. Edison also emphasized a highly standardized curriculum across schools that included the use of the Success for All reading curricula developed at Johns Hopkins University and the practically oriented Everyday Mathematics curriculum developed at the University of Chicago. This standardization would go so far as to have every Edison student in the nation learning the same subject at the same time. Edison schools would, if at all possible have no teachers' unions. As in the business world, teacher performance would be tied to student achievement measured by test scores. Teachers whose students did well on the tests would receive cash bonuses. As in the factory, teachers who did well in the classroom would be promoted to management and supervision where they would earn more. According to the plan, these innovations would guarantee quality and cut costs.

Business models of efficiency weighed heavily in the early Edison model. Student knowledge would be thoroughly measured by tests and quantified. Teacher efficiency at delivering knowledge would be measured by tests. Teacher and hence student output could be sped up with use of monetary incentives. As in the business world, nearly everything would be monitored, measured, and analyzed for greater and greater efficiency.

The early plans for Edison even involved the radical idea of students and parents heavily involved in administrative tasks and classroom assistance. Parental involvement in schooling and the seemingly progressive ideal of student involvement in self-governance appeared to coincide happily with the money-saving benefit to the company of hiring fewer teachers and administrators.

Today, most of Edison's early design has been abandoned. Most of what was abandoned was determined to be too expensive. The laptops that the company provided were never successfully integrated into lessons. Too few teachers and parents were able to help students use them. Many were broken. Despite that many Edison students are bilingual, dual-language instruction for all Edison students was abandoned as too costly. Although

Edison uses volunteer parents, student involvement in running the school was never integrated until 2002 when Whittle suggested that some financial losses of the school could be remedied by cutting administrators and replacing them with students. This met with a great deal of hostility from a number of parents and activists. Some aspects of the early model do remain, as I discuss more extensively in Chapter Two. The school day is slightly longer at Edison than at most public schools. Edison avoids teachers' unions wherever possible. Curriculum and schedules are much more highly standardized than in most school districts.

FORECAST

The popular press discussion and the academic discussion on Edison's rise and fall largely frame the issue in distinctly business terms of cost, efficacy of delivery defined through test performance, corruption, and the ineffectiveness of the public system. They also largely discuss public schooling in private terms of "accountability," "choice," "monopoly," "efficiency," and "competition," thereby confusing and collapsing the public possibilities for schooling with the private possibilities for the accumulation of profit. While I address the debates over test performance, finances, and corruption, this book contends that the most pressing issues about the Edison schools involve the role of public schooling in a democracy and more broadly the meaning of the privatization of the public sector in a democracy.

The success or failure of Edison is not so much about the alleged skills or alleged corruption of a group of business people as it is about the fundamental issues of school funding, the purpose of public schools, the role of teachers and administrators, the society's commitment to educating youth to become not merely consumers or disciplined workers but active participants in forging the future with the hope that they will make a better, more just, equal, and fair nation and world. As most critics note, Edison's primary concern with profitability comes at the expense of a focus on the quality of education. What distinguishes my discussion of Edison from the many other accounts is that I am not settling for the widely held belief that a quality education is one that merely offers individual students job opportunities or offers multinational corporations workers who have been trained at the public expense.

Part of the work of democracy involves transferring, to the public, power and control over deliberation and decision making about the future of society. This is evident in the public's reaction against Edison taking over their schools.

Edison Charter Academy, discussed in Chapter Three, is the only Edison school in San Francisco because the people of San Francisco acted together to challenge the district's contract with Edison. Citizens including students organized, protested, broke rules, got arrested, acted creatively, and engaged in spirited public dialogue in public space. Likewise, in Philadelphia, discussed in Chapter Four, students and other citizens also organized collectively and took to the street to challenge the Pennsylvania handover of the city schools to Edison.

> They chanted, "Hey, hey! Ho ho! Edison has got to go," and "It's not hard, it's not funny, all the other kids have money. Like the kids across the nation, we just want our education." To symbolize their desire to keep Edison out of the Philadelphia system, they grasped hands and formed a human chain around the entire building.[17]

Students held protest posters with statements such as "keep schools public." Collective action, frequently led by students, resulted in reconsideration by the governor of the plan to hand over the entire district of Philadelphia to the Edison Schools corporation. The noisy, messy, loud, creative, and distinctly democratic public action of citizens involved in debating the fate of public schools stands in stark contrast to the Edison model that, as the following chapters detail, involves disconnecting learning from broader social matters, standardizing learning, and pledging allegiance to the corporation.

As the fifth chapter discusses, public democratic renewal should not happen only in the streets but in the classroom too by linking learning to broader public problems and power struggles. Public democratic renewal promises that decisions about the future of political participation, economy, and culture are decisions that the vast majority of the population participates in making. The future of work and consumption, whose cultures and traditions matter and are legitimate — these should not be decisions reserved for a small number of wealthy citizens who currently control public and private resources and crucial knowledge-making institutions such as schools and mass media. Just as the consolidation of mass media into a few massive companies limits the possibility of dissenting and independent expression about matters of public import, so too the privatization of public schooling renders difficult if not impossible forms of schooling that challenge the amassing of private power at the expense of the public. In this sense, my criticisms of the Edison schools aim to be radically hopeful rather than sniping and cynical. Ultimately, I believe they point to what alternatives there are for strengthening public education in ways that imagine a future in which all schools are beacons of hope and all students represent the promise of a better world as they learn the intellectual skills to criticize and change it with others.

Although a number of interconnected scandals[18] have faced Edison (scandals that I address in the latter half of Chapter One), it would be a mistake to understand the problems with Edison as fundamentally problems with one company, one set of individual entrepreneurs, or one educational model. Rather, Edison is symptomatic of the privatization movement sweeping through multiple public sectors including health care, government work, and parks, to name a few. Although unbridled privatization has lost some of its shine in the wake of the collapse of Enron and WorldCom, these financial disasters have largely been framed in mass media as the results of accounting scandals or inept government management rather than as the basis for questioning whether it makes sense for essential public services and utilities such as energy, communications, and education to be subject to the whims of the market and the needs of investors. The misframing of events such as the Enron and WorldCom bankruptcies allows privatization enthusiasts in education to continue claiming that accountability comes from the fiscal discipline naturally accompanying privatization. However, in the wake of Enron, the radical decline of Edison stock, and the way public school teacher pension money was used to buy back Edison's stock (essentially using public money to bail out the private company),[19] the arguments of privatizers that the public sector is unfairly propped up ring more than a little hollow.

My recounting of the Edison story is meant to help readers start to consider what alternative pledges we should be making besides pledges to the corporation, and what schooling would look like if we were indeed to pledge differently. This book raises a number of questions about the project of privatizing public schools. But there is even more at stake in the Edison story than schooling. Chris Whittle's dream of reinventing U.S. public education with the market was part of a larger set of widely held beliefs about the public sector and the private sector. The story of Edison concerns much larger questions about the relationship between the public interest and the private accumulation of wealth, between what knowledge matters and who has the power to make it so, and between corporations and democracy.

1

THE RISE AND FALL

RISE

H. Christopher Whittle, a native of Tennessee and the son of a doctor, built a media empire that began in the early 1970s with a series of condensed textbooks at the University of Tennessee. While enrolled at the public university, Whittle and a friend paid graduate students to hone course textbooks down to essential information for the exam. These were called Time Savers. They later sold the business for a profit. In his next venture Whittle and friend Phillip Moffitt produced student guides called *Knoxville in a Nutshell*. Their company, which they named "13–30 Group" after the demographic they were targeting, produced these guides for incoming students and sought to profit by selling advertising to local businesses. Although *Knoxville in a Nutshell* made $2,000 initially, when they replicated the model at 20 universities they lost $160,000. Figuring they could make more with greater volume they started another 90 Nutshells. This put them into half a million dollars of debt as well as a frenzy to borrow from everyone they knew.[1]

When one Nutshell client, Nissan, asked Whittle how it could distinguish itself from other advertisers, Whittle came up with the idea of having a single-sponsor magazine. 13-30 Group shut down the Nutshells and produced a magazine called *America* featuring advertisement from only the Japanese automaker. Whittle's company became profitable again.

The company made other single-advertiser magazines as well as wall posters and sampler kits. In 1979, Whittle and Moffitt bought a floundering *Esquire* magazine. By 1986, they had "rebuilt the finances" of *Esquire* and decided to split.[2] By October 1988, Whittle launched his first solo project of the new Whittle Communications company, a magazine called *Special Reports* targeting mothers in the waiting rooms of fifteen thousand obstetrician-gynecologists, pediatricians, and family doctors. The unique element of *Special Reports* was the contract clause demanding that doctors not subscribe to more than two other magazines for the waiting rooms. Whittle planned on enforcing this exclusivity through spot checks. Whittle Communications was involved in a number of innovative advertisement-based businesses in the 1980s. For example, Whittle was leading the way at putting closed circuit television into doctor's waiting rooms. Whittle Communications would sell advertising time to companies that could be assured that the patients in the waiting room could not change the channel or leave the room. By 1988, Whittle Communications had sales of $106 million and 900 employees with numerous advertising and publishing enterprises.

According to N. R. Kleinfield of *The New York Times*, Whittle was "the company's main idea man and main salesman," coming up with about a third of the company's ideas.[3] Whittle's strengths appear to lie in raising investment capital, sales, and visualizing grand projects. Former Whittle employee, decade-long CEO of Conde Nast Publishing, and former president of *New Yorker* magazine, Steven Florio described Whittle as "probably the most brilliant salesman I've met."[4] Florio is less complimentary on the content of Whittle's publications, describing *Special Reports* as "fair at best." Kleinfield writes:

> Like the contents of other Whittle publications, the editorial quality of Special Reports has taken some heat. "They're clean and neat, but they don't feel real," said Mr. Lipstein [founder of American Health magazine]. "I don't happen to think they're good."[5]

Whittle's business successes in the 1980s culminated in his creation of Channel One. Channel One is a classroom news program found today in 350,000 public school classrooms airing to more than eight million school kids (though it is now owned by Primedia). In exchange for televisions and VCRs, estimated by the company to be valued at $50,000, schools would agree to play the programming in the mornings. The programming contains commercials that target market school kids — products like Snickers, Levi's, and Head & Shoulders shampoo. Channel One was an unprecedented success at making kids a captive audience for junk food, clothing, and other products. Channel One also brought Whittle to national attention as press coverage highlighted public outrage over the plans to make public school students watch commercials. *The New York Times* described the controversy this way:

> Though advocates have applauded it as a crafty way to interest students in current affairs, the project has been criticized by some educators as an "appalling idea" and an "advertising Valhalla," and there have been calls for "Whittle-free zones."[6]

On the way to creating the Edison schools, Whittle had some major financial triumphs, like the sale to Time, Inc. of half of Whittle Communications for $185 million (of which he received $40 million). By 1989, Whittle Communications was involved in 42 projects that had not attracted the kind of national attention garnered by Channel One.[7] These projects included the magazines: Go! Girls Only!, Dental Health Advisor, and Pet Care Report, and Funnies wall posters.[8] Whittle also had some serious flops on the way to Edison, such as his attempt to create a magazine for boys that aimed to follow his successful Go!, which was a profitable magazine for girls 11-14. Go! stood for "Girls Only!" He created a counterpart magazine for boys titled BANG! It was subtitled "Boys and Not Girls."

> When editors unveiled the test mock-up at a Muscatine, Iowa, school the eleven- and twelve-year-old pupils giggled. One boy read the logo and subtitle as a sentence. "Bang boys and not girls?" he smirked. "I don't think the principal would okay that!"[9]

Although not every business venture was a success, Whittle did have a distinctive talent for seeing commercial potential in places that had been considered out of bounds for business.

WHITTLE'S INNOVATION: COMMERCIALIZING PUBLIC SPACE

Despite Whittle's comparison of the Edison schools to the innovations of Thomas Edison, unlike Thomas Edison, Whittle has made no noteworthy invention. Whittle's business acumen has largely involved finding ways of transforming public institutions and resources into private for-profit opportunities. Whittle's specialty has been what The New York Times called "the commercialization of the sacrosanct."[10] At Whittle Communications, Whittle was scheming to get advertising into not just schools but churches and onto the appliances in people's homes. Whittle has almost no compunctions about where you can put advertising, and thus in propagating his projects he has tapped into some raw emotions.[11] For Whittle, apparently no space is off-limits for advertising and profit. No space is sacred. Literally.

> Whittle and Rinker Buck, the editorial director of AdWeek's Marketing Week, were meeting to get to know one another better. Whittle had made the overture because he had been miffed at some rather blistering coverage in Buck's publication. Whittle sipped a drink, as Buck spun an anecdote that had to do with keeping recipes on his refrigerator.
> "We've thought of ads on refrigerators," Whittle interrupted.
> Buck laughed.
> It was not a joke.
> In fact, Whittle later told me, the company had thought of trying to interest a maker like Whirlpool into building frames for wall media on its refrigerators, and then homeowners could pick up the material at the supermarket and slide it in.
> Buck lit into Whittle on Channel One. He told Whittle how irritating it is to watch commercial-ridden Saturday-morning television with his 5-year-old daughter.
> "Advertising is making available a good program," Whittle said. "It is a trade-off."
> After some back and forth, Buck said, "Listen, you're an alternative medium. You consider the high schools a segment. Have you considered the churches?"
> Slight embarrassment prickled his face, but Whittle just laughed. (Later on, he told me he had not ruled out churches, but could not think of anything he might do there.)[12]

Although Whittle may consider every space fair game for advertising, it has been particularly public spaces that he has sought to commercialize in his careers in marketing, publishing, and education. Whittle's successes in school commercialism and privatization need to be understood in relation to school funding. The cuts to federal funding of public schooling as a percentage of federal spending began in 1980 with the Reagan Administration and continue to the present.[13] Despite the rhetoric of the Bush Administration about increased funding for schools tied to No Child Left Behind (NCLB), as of 2004 federal education programs have received the smallest increases in six years and schools charged with raising achievement by NCLB will receive $7 billion less than what the law called for.[14] Desperation for resources to maintain the quality of schools has driven administrators and school boards to open the schools to advertisers who know how important it is to build brand loyalty by targeting kids and "imprinting" brand awareness at the earliest age. Cuts to school funding have not only opened the door to advertisers but have also been central to the calls to privatize "failing schools." The opportunities for profit that have resulted from undermining the funding of one of America's most important public resources had not been lost on Chris Whittle.

"SAVING" PUBLIC SCHOOLS WITH THE MARKET

> After Channel One, Whittle realized that, as he put it, "running schools is the heart of the game."[15]

In the early 1990s as Channel One was facing heavy criticism and Whittle and his new CEO Benno Schmidt were trying to expand Edison, Schmidt was making appearances to defend the plan for Edison. On the *Today* show Schmidt faced the principal of Washington's Hine Junior High School, who described the Edison idea as "a travesty against children." A follow-up exchange between Schmidt and renowned education author Jonathan Kozol offers greater insight into the underlying ideal behind Edison.

> The Edison Project, Kozol said, is "the first nail in the coffin of public education as we've known it for 150 years.... I mean, you don't help the public schools by starting private schools. If you want to improve the public's water supply, you don't do it by selling champagne."
>
> Schmidt responded gravely, saying he shared Kozol's views about inequities in education. Then for some reason, he fed Kozol what he thought was a rhetorical question about the virtues of entrepreneurship: "I think you need to ask," Schmidt said, "if you want to reform the post office, would you try to work within it or would you start Federal Express."
>
> Kozol pounced: "Ah, but that's a very good example. The fact is that only affluent people use Federal Express.... I use Fed Ex, and you probably do too, but the poor people of America never use Federal Express, and the post office has deteriorated as a result."[16]

This exchange illustrates the debate over strengthening public schools versus abandoning the public dimension of public schooling in favor of redefining public schooling through business metaphors and elitism.

The origins of Edison logically extend "the commercialization of the sacrosanct." Whittle's dream may not have been without good intentions. The origins of Edison date to a speech that Whittle tested out on the East Tennessee Teachers Association in the fall of 1989 that he gave days later to the Tennessee Business Roundtable.[17] What was innovative in Whittle's approach was the shifting of public school debate away from traditional terms of equity, public service, the common good, and individual edification and toward the language of business.

In glowing terms Whittle described what he called "The New American School." Using a series of flamboyant metaphors from space exploration to chariot racing, Whittle called for authoritative federal government action to remake American public schooling radically. It is remarkable how much of Whittle's early vision for Edison is at odds with what would become the Edison schools. Consider these progressive ideas that Whittle later jettisoned: students should learn why they should learn; there should be no tests; there should be no homework in the ideal New American School; the new school would cut student/teacher ratios by relying on students learning from other students; students would learn from assistant teachers — the young people and elderly people who could be a part of a new national service corps; schools would be open year round and offer day care; each student would have a computer and teachers would have private offices and telephones. Part of the radical plan aimed for "efficiency" and cost-cutting by students taking on the roles of teachers and administrators.

> As he told Schmidt, on the same $5,500 that American taxpayers currently spend per student annually, the schools should turn a profit of 12 to 15 percent. Later the Whittle enterprise would make money by selling the educational software and other services it would have developed to public schools. "We can reduce costs in many ways," Chris told Schmidt. "Elimination of bureaucracy, introduction of technology.... We see parents and students doing many things that would lower tuition. Not just cafeteria and janitorial work, but students teaching students, for instance."[18]

This ideal of "innovative" school design would later come back to haunt Edison in 2002 as Edison appeared to be on the verge of financial death and Whittle proposed replacing administrators with school kids to save money.

While media attention has focused on Edison's extravagant use of funds at a staff conference, advocates say Whittle's remarks show the company is morally unfit and philosophically mismatched for its educational mission. Whittle had directly connected the use of student workers to cost-cutting measures for schools, commenting that 600 pupils working one hour a day was the equivalent of 75 full-time adult staff. He had suggested that such an action could be in place by 2004. Janet McCoy, a 6th grader at the Edison-run Gillespie Middle School, said she was angry about the suggestion. "It's wrong for them to use students as free labor when we come to school to learn," McCoy said. McCoy pointed out that money is needed for books and qualified teachers, saying she still lacks history textbooks in her classes. Parents and community members said the suggestion was the equivalent of child labor, noting that the majority of Edison's students are elementary-aged.[19]

Whittle's proposal certainly raises questions whether the original "innovative" ideas were nothing more than schemes to run schools as cheaply as possible under the guise of introducing "progressive" teaching methods. In any case, as the next chapter details, Edison would come to abandon nearly all of these "innovative" designs that were supposed to make Edison unique.

One of Whittle's listeners at the Business Roundtable speech in the fall of 1989 was president of the University of Tennessee, future secretary of education under the first George Bush, and future presidential candidate Lamar Alexander. Whittle's phrase "New American School" would end up a catchphrase in the administration's education policy rhetoric. In the speech, Whittle called on the president of the United States to give a billion dollars to fund research into reinventing American education and opening 50 new model schools:

Just as it took the federal government to guide us through the depression, to rally us to war, to fund the Manhattan Project,

> to inspire our interstate highways, it will require the federal government to create the blueprint for the New American School ... I did not say build it or run it. The idea of the federal government running our schools is about as appealing as a federally-run fast-food chain. I said redesign it.[20]

Whittle's call for massive federal funding for business-led school reform coincided closely with the plan of the George H. W. Bush Administration.

> Announcement of the Edison Project came close on the heels of a strikingly similar "America 2000" plan launched by the Bush administration as its new strategy to overhaul the nation's schools. At President George Bush's behest, two dozen top business executives organized the New American Schools Development Corporation as a catalyst for educational reform, undertaking to raise $200 million from concerns such as Exxon, Boeing, AT&T, and Xerox. From this fund Education Secretary Lamar Alexander intended to issue research and development grants to the private sector for projects to invent 535 new public schools that would serve as models of excellence and could be replicated nationwide.[21]

Whittle declined to apply for the money that the administration was making available. Vance Trimble and the *Knoxville News-Sentinel* suggest that this had to do with Whittle avoiding conflict of interest accusations for prior financial dealings with Alexander.[22] For example, in addition to catchy phrases like "New American School," money had been transferred from Whittle to Lamar Alexander and to Alexander's wife, Honey. Alexander received sweet consulting fees of $125,000 for Whittle's now defunct *Tennessee Illustrated* magazine. Alexander also bought four shares of Whittle Communications for $10,000 in 1987. One year later when Time, Inc. bought half of Whittle's enterprise, Whittle bought back the four shares from Alexander for $330,000. These shares had been issued in Honey's name. Lamar Alexander's involvement with Edison continued through Tom Ingram, a Nashville former newspaper reporter, editor of *Nashville* magazine, and business consultant.

> [Ingram] not only had been his [Alexander's] campaign manager and chief of staff as Tennessee governor but had also helped Alexander in assembling his Washington staff when he left the presidency of the University of Tennessee to join the Bush cabinet.[23]

In 1991, Whittle planned to build 1,000 new, for-profit schools, 200 of them within five years, at a projected cost of $2.5 billion. That year Whittle announced that Edison would be putting together a small transitional team of executives to establish a more permanent organization and plan for the staff and project:

> The primary need was for someone with a sufficient grasp of education to take day-to-day charge of coordinating Whittle schools until the core team of innovators, whom Whittle termed education's Mercury Astronauts, could be chosen and in place with their own staff — by January 1992. The job went to Tom Ingram.[24]

This was not Whittle's first acquaintance with Ingram. Ingram, while working as a business consultant, had been referred to Whittle by Lamar Alexander to help Whittle decide whether or not to launch a career as a politician in 1987. Later, as *Special Reports* was doing poorly, Whittle would put Ingram in as the chief executive. Whittle's selection of someone experienced in politics, business, and media but not education to head the initial Edison planning group may be seen as indicative of Edison's priorities.

The "Mercury Astronauts" of education that Tom Ingram picked for the Edison planning stage at the beginning of 1992 would turn out to be mostly a mix of media specialists and conservative advocates of privatizing public schools: John Chubb from the conservative Brookings Institute; Chester Finn, an education professor at Vanderbilt University and former assistant secretary of education in the Reagan and first Bush Administrations; Sylvia Peters, a Chicago principal who had been hailed as a hero for "leading parents and activists to build a safe haven for her pupils in a crime infested neighborhood"; former *Esquire* editor and assistant managing editor of *Newsweek* Dominique Browning; another media expert, writer, and producer, Nancy Hechinger; and Daniel Beiderman of the Grand Central and 34th Street Partnerships in New York City, who was an expert on raising public financing for private endeavors.

As I discuss in Chapter Two, the New American School organization continued during the George W. Bush Administration to influence both the Edison curriculum and the national curriculum agenda. This early relationship between Edison and conservative policy ideologists and conservative politicians would only intensify as early Whittle supporters included some of the nation's highest profile governors and mayors. These early supporters included Secretary of Homeland Security and former Pennsylvania governor Tom Ridge, who as governor would attempt to hand the running of the Philadelphia public schools over to Edison; Rudolph "America's Mayor" Giuliani, who would attempt to privatize New York City's higher education remediation programs and bring in Edison's Benno Schmidt to lead a review to justify it; Massachusetts governor William Weld, who would invest in Edison and then join an investment firm oriented toward educational privatization initiatives that would profit from both the Edison initial public stock offering and the stock buyback. Both Giuliani and Weld, respectively, would use connections made while in office to invest in private for-profit schooling as soon as they left office. The origins of Edison involved not only conservative ideologists in politics but in academia too.

LURING BENNO

Whittle's success in expanding the Edison Project owed in no small part to his ability to lure President of Yale University Benno C. Schmidt, Jr. Schmidt's father, also named Benno Schmidt, was a multimillionaire venture capitalist who was a partner in investment firm J. H. Whitney. Schmidt, Sr., was described in 1980 in a *Washington Post* article on a high-society ball as a member of the "crème de la crème of the scientific/academic/and business world,"[25] alongside the chairs of companies including PepsiCo, DuPont, US Steel, and Uniroyal. After he died in 1999, his luxurious, 12-room Manhattan apartment made the news when it was sold for a record price of close to $8.1 million. Benno Schmidt, Jr., married Helen Whitney. Coming from the presidency of Yale between 1986 and 1992 and a prior deanship at Columbia law school, as well as having clerked for Supreme Court Chief Justice Earl Warren, Schmidt's pedigree and credentials conferred to Edison a necessary legitimacy.

Trimble recounts the following from his interviews with Benno Schmidt on the subject of how Whittle wooed him from his position at Yale:

> "I heard," Schmidt recalls, "more of his conception of how the project would be organized and conceived from the beginning, what his strategy was for thinking that it could be accomplished, what his public purposes were in doing it. This was really intended by him as an effort to kind of open up a system of education that he felt was closed and increasingly moribund and failing. And his view that opening it up to innovation and

competition and choice was probably the best way to bring about change that was crucial."[26]

When Schmidt joined Edison, original plans for the company involved opening a chain of elite for-profit academies that would likely have been funded by a national voucher scheme supported by the first Bush Administration. The scheme would have allowed public tax money to be doled out to parents who could then shop for private schools with public money and possibly subsidize the vouchers. Original plans for publicly funded private academies coincided more with Schmidt's elite background and upbringing than did the plan that developed when Congress did not support vouchers. Critics worried that the Edison schools would cash in on the privatization initiative by catering to the high-end education market:

> There are those who say that Whittle's schools will be elitist institutions, open only to those who can pay the price. He has tried to counter this by promising to have some scholarships and a couple of schools open to inner-city youngsters.... Still it is unlikely that his schools will enroll students who need special, expensive education. Few schools will be in ghettos, where education faces its most daunting challenge.... Although Whittle contends his system would not depend on vouchers, he would naturally benefit if President Bush is able to persuade Congress to enact a voucher system, at least on a trial basis.[27]

Although vouchers did not take off as hoped, the charter school movement did.

Charter school contracts tend to allow public schools to operate without a number of requirements typically demanded of public school systems. Charter schools were generally an experimental approach in poorer districts. The acceleration of the charter school movement meant opportunities for Edison to change tack and run urban, largely nonwhite public schools. Although Edison would not aim to open elite private schools but rather run public schools in the poorest communities, Edison benefited by the popular association of for-profit schooling with the kind of elite boarding schools that someone like Schmidt might attend. In the press Whittle and Schmidt appeared to seldom miss a chance to describe public schools in terms such as "failing" and "moribund."

In one of the early meetings between Whittle and Schmidt, Schmidt asked about the name. Trimble recounts:

> Schmidt was curious about the name — Edison Project.
>
> "Edison did not tinker with candles to make them burn better," says Chris Whittle. "Instead, he created something brilliantly new: the light bulb. In the same fashion, American education needs a fundamental breakthrough, a new dynamic that will light the way to a transformed educational system."[28]

This exchange between Whittle and Schmidt illuminates more than it appears to. Contrary to Whittle's promotional statements and contrary to popular belief, Edison did not invent the light bulb. He perfected it by improving the vacuum inside the globe, decreasing the electrical current, and refining the filament by tirelessly experimenting with multiple materials for it.[29] The electric light bulb had been around for fifty years.

I do not want to downplay the importance and brilliance of Thomas Edison who invented among other things recorded sound, motion picture, and perhaps most significantly a system for producing and distributing inexpensive electrical power. While Thomas Edison's scientific innovations are legendary in scope and importance, in fact, Edison's scientific innovations were nearly matched by his genius for patenting and self-promotion. Thomas Edison held a record for patents, holding more than 1,000 in his lifetime, and he sued those who he thought infringed. As well, Thomas Edison's company, Thomas Edison Incorporated (which is now General Electric), was at the forefront of the rise of the modern corporation. It bought up smaller companies, used investment companies for financing and management, and Thomas Edison created the first research park. However, Thomas Edison did not revel in the industrial transformations of the early twentieth century that displaced the independent inventor, craftsperson, tinkerer, and mechanic for the scientist, engineer, and the salaried corporate worker. Technological innovation became increasingly dependent on the financial sector for an invention to be made into a salable commodity. As sociologist and labor historian Stanley Aronowitz explains, Thomas Edison "never ceased to rue his demise under the hammer of the corporate form of industrial organization."[30] The point not to be missed here is that despite Whittle's use of Edison's name to associate corporate schooling with innovation and inspiration, Edison himself did not view the corporate form of industrial organization as auspicious to innovation and invention. The truth about Thomas Edison mattered less for marketing the company than the quintessential advertiser's use of the image and associations that the name conferred. Like Benno Schmidt, Thomas Edison served as an important symbol in Whittle's permanent promotional campaign to sell the Edison schools. Schmidt was not the only prominent academic involved in the origins of Edison.

At about the same time that the Edison Project was born, John Chubb (who would become Edison's Chief Educational Officer), with Terry Moe, wrote a groundbreaking book on educational policy titled *Politics, Markets, and America's Schools*, which would be the first major argument that "democracy" in education is facilitated better by markets than by political participation.[31] Chubb explained it more recently in a book edited by Moe that brings together noted right-wing scholars who bash teachers, teacher unions, public schools, and the public sector while celebrating markets, business, and businesspeople as more ethical, efficient, and accountable. (The book was published by the conservative and heavily financed Hoover Institution.)

> There are other ways the country could provide free and universal public education, accountable to democratic authorities.... The new system would be subject less to the principles of politics and more to the principles of the market ... market control would begin by transferring the authority to operate schools from local school boards exclusively to other providers, approved by democratic authorities. New providers would be funded not by administrative convenience but by enrollment. New providers would need to enroll students to remain in business, pressure that should encourage schools to do whatever is necessary as effectively as possible to attract and maintain students.[32]

Considering the business-driven vision of Whittle and Schmidt, it was no coincidence that John Chubb and Chester Finn, Jr., the biggest academic boosters of shifting the school reform debates to business terms and concerns, would end up working for Whittle. Finn would participate in the earliest planning stage of the company and Chubb would become the Chief Education Officer. These privatization advocates described public schooling as a business and used business terminology of "monopoly," "choice," "competition," "efficiency," "accountability," and "failure" to describe schools. For example, the public sector had a "monopoly" on schools that prevented "competition," which would lead to "efficiency" and "accountability." Subject the public schools to the same kinds of pressures that businesses face, so went the argument, and the public schools will benefit from a kind of fiscal-based discipline.

This market language obscures the purpose of public schooling. Public schools are not businesses and they do not aim to accumulate profits. While ideally public schools should prepare students for work, they also have a public role of preparing students to participate in running the society they live in. That purpose has been wholly absent from the rhetoric of the proprivatization crowd, and with good reason. The privatizers have a view of society that elevates the private accumulation of profit to the highest principle. This means that for privatizers the role of education is (1) to enable students to have an opportunity to compete for jobs in a corporate-dominated economy and (2) to serve as worker training so that U.S corporations can compete in the global economy. Not only were these goals made quite explicit by the privatizers and their academic cheerleaders at the time of Edison's inception, but they had already been formulated during the Reagan Administration with the *A Nation at Risk* report.

This singular view of schooling as an economic enterprise for the student and the nation has come to replace the democratic tradition of schooling for civic participation and for students to learn the tools to make society a more ethical place.

In addition to reducing the political and ethical possibilities of schooling to allegedly neutral market mechanisms,[33] another problem with the market-based description of public schooling embraced by Whittle and the privatizers is that it wrongly assumes that laissez-faire economic principles naturally result in efficiencies. This is hardly the case.

Since the Great Depression, all industrialized nations have relied on state subsidies to make sure that technological development and economic stability could be assured. These subsidies take different forms in different nations. Whereas Japan and Korea have developed economically through agencies that coordinate state economic stimulus with conglomerate corporations, in the United States the subsidies are sometimes overt (the truly massive agriculture subsidies) and sometimes masked (the Pentagon transfers public wealth to high-tech industry). Despite rhetoric of the virtues of free trade, the United States demands liberalization of trade of third-world countries yet frequently does not follow the same discipline (the World Trade Organization scuffle in 2003 over unfair U.S. steel tariffs is a case in point, as well as the breakup of the free trade talks in Cancun over the issue of U.S. subsidized agriculture). High protectionism and coordinated economic planning have been central to all nations that have enjoyed economic development. Yet free trade and privatization are demanded by the United States of Africa, Latin America, the Caribbean, the Pacific Rim, and other regions that, were they to develop economically, would damage their present role in providing cheap labor and markets for the United States. The point here is that the business metaphors that form the basis for the privatizers' arguments do not correspond to the ways markets really work. To be even more blunt here, before privatizing public education, let us see what happens to businesses across the U.S. economy without public sector assistance in the form of tax credits, subsidies, loans, and laws protecting capital interests.

Advocates of privatization often rely on economic metaphors as well as racial and gender metaphors for their arguments. The metaphor of discipline that educational privatizers invoke to call for turning public schools that have been shortchanged by the school funding structure into markets for the rich is not only disingenuous in terms of real economic activity; it also carries a charged racial implication. Mainstream discussion of global economics and urban poverty tend to blame the victims, respectively, nonwhite third-world citizens and the predominantly nonwhite urban poor, by attributing to them a lack of moral character, a lack of individual discipline. The supposed hard discipline of a market that just so happens to be controlled by white guys will provide a remedy. As well, the language of privatization scapegoats women by suggesting that urban schools have suffered by being dominated by women teachers who lack the "hard discipline" that the market "naturally" provides. Furthermore, the language of discipline intersects with the sexist accusation that the failures of urban public schooling have less to do with institutionalized poverty, corporate plunder, and systematic white supremacy, than with the parental failure of single mothers, deadbeat parents, or female teachers with whom the final responsibility for education lies.[34] I raise these facts not to bash white guys but rather to point to the ways that privatization advocates rely heavily upon racist and sexist assumptions, stereotypes, metaphors, and representations to further their goals of bashing public schools.

Chubb's call for public schools to be privatized and dependent on "consumer demand," that is, student enrollment, to stay in "business" does not make sense considering that nineteen Edison schools nationwide have had their contracts revoked because of such problems as low test scores, high teacher turnover rates, and disputes over the leadership and accountability of the company. Chubb would no doubt claim that his company has provided nothing less than the best educational services a private company could offer. What if no company can do better than Edison? Parents would not have a choice of another provider and there would be no pressure on a company like Edison to improve. Would other companies rush into the education industry when Edison has never made a profit? Advocates of privatization claim that all of the failures of educational privatization owe to the impositions and agenda of public school bureaucrats. However, as subsequent chapters in this book illustrate, problems in the Edison schools with high teacher turnover, inexperienced teachers, overworked and underpaid teachers, financial problems, instability, and questionable testing practices appear to derive principally from privatization and its pressures.

By 1993, Whittle had reduced the scope of the planned Edison Project, from opening a network of private schools, to managing 20 public schools. Although Whittle Communications secured about $40 million from two major investors, Philips Electronics NV and Associated Newspaper Holdings. Time Warner, Inc., an initial investor, refused to put any more money toward the project.

Although Chris Whittle conceived the idea for Edison in the late 1980s, by the time he made public his model for the Edison schools his magazine and media empire were collapsing around him in the early 1990s. He had been forced out of his magazine business, had lost his business selling medical patients as a captive audience to advertisers, and was so desperate to finance what was originally called The Edison Project that he sold his homes and art collection to help do so.[35]

Nearly a decade before the spectacular collapses of Enron and WorldCom and the return of accusations of accounting irregularities that would face Edison Schools, Whittle Communications was accused of "aggressive accounting practices" that resulted in "a significant overstatement of Channel One's revenue."[36] "When Channel One failed to sell all its commercial time, extra spots for advertisers like Mars Inc. and Pepsico were run and accounted for as current revenue, overstating actual revenue in one instance by nearly 20 percent."[37] The accounting scandal revealed that Whittle may have had a penchant for creativity with more than big ideas. "'Even inside the company, you were always trying to get a handle on what was real and what wasn't,' Mr. Belis said yesterday. The mantra was, 'Are these Whittle numbers or real numbers?'"[38]

In *Business Week,* Mr. Schmidt was quoted as saying that Mr. Whittle "hasn't been involved at all in day-to-day activities" at Edison.... Edison might be "the greatest" of Mr. Whittle's illusions, ... because Whittle's financial failings mean that "the likelihood at this juncture of major investors trusting their capital" to him "seems remote."... "An even more fundamental drawback," the [*New Yorker*] article states, "is that once the public-school administrators of America have absorbed the magnitude" of Mr. Whittle's "failure with his other ventures, they are hardly likely to trust him with their tax dollars, let alone their children."[39]

Both Pulitzer prize–winning business author Vance Trimble and *The New York Times* education journalist Diana Henriques paint a picture of Whittle as a man who is a natural salesman but not terribly skilled as a manager. In fact, both suggest that as Whittle Communications was falling apart, Whittle was "living a princely life," had recruited talented but inexperienced people, and was spending at a rate alarming to investors. In 1994, as Whittle was trying to raise money for Edison, investors forced his removal from position as chief executive of Whittle Communications[40] and liquidated "corporate jets, lavish furnishings and palatial headquarters."

After the board removed Whittle, the incoming CEO of Whittle Communications cut *Special Reports* and the TV version Medical News Network. Channel One was sold to K-III Communications. Whittle Communications major investors Time Warner and Phillips lost $120 million and $175 million, respectively. With the demise of Whittle Communications by 1994, Whittle was able to hold on to little more than his stake in the Edison Project. Whittle's stake in the company and his personal fortune were unclear. Trimble writes:

Just what the end of the dream did to Chris financially is not clear. "I don't know exactly what I made," Chris says. "But I made profits over the years. One way to look at it is, if you were in the first twenty years you did fine. It was the last three or four that hurt." For many years Whittle's top executives shared another benefit — a princely life-style with first class or private jet travel, $500-hotel suites, leased Porsches, and salaries thought to range from $400,000 to $800,000.[41]

As Whittle Communications was heading toward fiscal crisis, work had continued on the creation of the $55 million Georgian-style headquarters in Knoxville. The American taxpaying public ended up buying the Whittle Communications campus and transforming it into a federal courthouse, thereby keeping Whittle Communications from entering bankruptcy. Although it avoided bankruptcy there was essentially nothing left of Whittle Communications other than the Edison plans after the cuts and sell-offs to eliminate the debt accrued by Chris Whittle's leadership. Nearly all of the early planners in the Edison Project left the company.

Despite the financial successes of Channel One, Whittle Communications was not able to remain profitable. In part this had to do with Whittle's ambitious attempts to expand the company rapidly. A number of articles appeared in the popular and business press detailing the collapse of Whittle Communications. Famed business writer James B. Stewart broke the story in October 1994 in an article titled "Grand Illusion." The Grand Illusion was one of profitability for the company.

> "The amazing thing is he escaped serious scrutiny for so long," Gary Belis, Whittle's former media relations director, said yesterday. "Chris Whittle had a remarkable ability to get smart people to do stupid things," added Mr. Belis, who left Whittle late in 1991 and is now corporate publicity director at Wenner Media in New York.[42]

As Whittle Communications was spiraling downward, it was revealed that the company failed to pay state personal property taxes on hundreds of thousands of VCRs and TV sets that it used for Channel One. The company did not file tax returns in many states that require them. Whittle faced more than $10 million in unpaid taxes and penalties.

> Those liabilities were a reason that the K-III Communications Corporation, which agreed in August to buy Channel One from Whittle, has reduced the purchase price to $240 million from $300 million ... and insisted on indemnification.[43]

At the end of 1994, plans for The Edison Project were in trouble. Investor Time Warner fled, leaving Chris Whittle (with 20 percent), Philips Electronics (with 40 percent), and Associated Newspapers (with 40 percent). Associated Newspapers had already invested so many millions of dollars that the company "felt they had to continue to gamble, even though the plan to reinvent American education still looked difficult."[44] Both Philips and Associated gave a strict deadline to Whittle to come up with investment capital or they would pull out of Edison, thereby guaranteeing its demise. The project needed between $25 million and $75 million to guarantee the Edison launch. "Wiring one school for a video-computer network was estimated at $800,000."[45] When Whittle put up $24 million of his own money, it shifted ownership and he now shared a third of the company with Philips and Associated. He still needed more money.

Investment bankers Dillon, Reed were working for Edison, trying to convince investors to put money in an education company that had not yet opened a single school and that had been the only piece left of what was Whittle Communications. An investment firm named Sprout took interest in Edison. Senior partner Janet Hickey negotiated a last-minute contract with Edison that Whittle and Schmidt brought to Philips. Whittle was going to liquidate his personal assets, buy out Philips and Associated, and take over total control of Edison in exchange for a payment of $30 million in seven weeks. By early 1995, $30 million was set up in financing for Edison with $15 million coming from Whittle's holding company, $12 million from Sprout, and the remaining $3 million from Edison executive

Benno Schmidt and two of his friends, Joel Smilow, chairman of Playtex, and John W. Childs.[46] The agreement involved cutting the first wave of startup schools from 20 to only 4, and it also involved cutting the salaries of the executives from top corporate salaries typical of Fortune 50 companies to ones more commensurate with a company that had no revenue. Edison's overhead was also slashed. Whittle's success at expanding Edison could not have continued without this financing. The first Edison schools opened in Boston, Sherman, Texas, Wichita, Kansas, and Mount Clemens, Michigan.

By November 1996, Edison was running 12 schools and was involved in the third major solicitation of private financing of $30.5 million. This brought to $100 million the money raised by Edison since its inception. Investors in this round included Richmont Leeds Education Company LLC; J.W. Childs Associates, LP; Zesiger Capital Group LLC; and Christopher Whittle, who remained the company's largest equity holder.

By the fall of 1997, Edison was managing 25 schools, most of which were part of larger school districts. It began to start charter schools, which would give the company significantly more autonomy over the schools it manages. Edison claimed to have spent $45 million on curriculum development and the school model and announced it would seek $50 million from the private equity market. The company considered an initial public offering of stock in hopes of raising $75 million to-$100 million necessary for continued expansion.

By the following year, Edison was running 51 schools nationwide enrolling more than 24,000 students in 26 communities. The company announced that it would be offering teachers limited stock options the next year when the company would become publicly traded. Chris Cerf, Edison's executive vice president, announced that the company would expand the next year to add 22 schools.

Cerf reports that the expansion would bring Edison to "static-state profitability," the point at which the company would become profitable if it stopped growth expenditures. In October, the Edison Project obtains $56 million of private equity financing, bringing the total raised since 1991 to $161 million. Two companies, J.P. Morgan Capital Corporation and Investor AB of Sweden, invested $20 million each, with the remainder coming from WSI Inc. (a holding company controlled by Chris Whittle) and Richmont Leeds Education Company, an education industry investment corporation. With the new financing, Edison projected that by 2001 it will increase the number of schools it manages to 75.[47]

In 1999, Edison was launched as a publicly traded company on Nasdaq. Leeds Weld facilitated the IPO.

Despite steady expansion by 2000 the first major problems become evident in press coverage of Edison, foreshadowing a whirlwind of crisis and scandal that would come to a head in 2002. The Evaluation Center at Western Michigan University published the first major study of Edison, finding its performance does not live up to the promises that the company makes to school districts. Teachers at Edison Charter Academy in San Francisco threatened a walkout over extensive unpaid overtime. In 2000, Boston Renaissance, Edison's "Flagship School," renewed its contract for five years only to cancel it the following year after poor test score results and disputes between the company and local administrators over control.

In 2001, the SEC (Securities and Exchange Commission) charged that Edison failed to disclose that as much as 41 percent of its 2001 revenue consisted of money that it never saw: $154 million of the $376 million in revenue Edison reported consists of district-paid employee expenses.[48] Things looked good for Edison when the State of Pennsylvania hired Edison to study the Philadelphia public schools and to recommend a course of action to reform one of the nation's largest urban school districts. Edison's stock price peaked at more than $36 per share, about twice the issuing price.

After Edison's report recommended turning over control of the Philadelphia school district to for-profit and other managers, Pennsylvania promised Edison 60 of 240 public schools to run as well as the management of the city school district. This stood to be the largest experiment in public school privatization in history. Although Wall Street liked the idea, citizens, students, parents, and unions protested the decision. Edison was not given a contract to manage the district and instead received twenty rather than 60 schools to run. Wall Street reacted and Edison's stock price plummeted reaching 97¢ per share. Desperate for financing for the upcoming school year, Edison borrowed $40 million at interest rates in the teens. Desperate for cost-cutting, Chris Whittle proposed replacing experienced administrators with students. Generally favorable press coverage turned against Edison with a number of commentators predicting the end not only of Edison but of the public school privatization movement.[49]

PUBLIC RELATIONS

Whittle had learned his lesson from his experience with Channel One about the importance of using careful public relations tactics in announcing his intentions. When he wheeled out Channel One in the 1980s, Whittle was attacked in the press, by teachers' unions, educational specialists, and others who were aghast at an unprecedented attempt at selling kids to advertisers. So when breaking the secrecy of the early "Mercury Astronaut" planning and rolling out Edison to the public, Whittle first contacted the American Federation of Teachers and the National Education Association. Edison was met by surprisingly mild criticism by these unions despite the fact that Edison's plans involved hiring non-unionized teachers, circumventing the certification process, and taking advantage of the growing charter school movement that would, in some cases, allow it to hire non-unionized and uncertified teachers.

The lack of aggressive early opposition to Edison on the part of the unions owes less to their failure to represent teachers adequately than it does to the extent to which public–private "partnerships" have come to be viewed as unquestionably beneficial to everybody. For example, the principal ways that corporations have managed to infiltrate schools with advertisements on school walls, school buses, in the textbooks, on scoreboards, and with exclusive vending contracts have had a lot to do not only with the schools being underfunded and hence in need of cash but also with the cultural shift that has encouraged administrators and teachers to think of working with the "corporate community" as prestigious. In exchange for getting a highly impressionable captive audience for lucrative brand exposure, the corporations offer the schools their "partnership." Another interrelated dimension of the reason unions were slow to oppose Edison involves the extent to which conservative thought captured common sense and overtook the political climate and culture from the election of Ronald Reagan in 1980 through the administrations of the first George Bush and Bill Clinton. During this period conservatives succeeded in building think tanks, mass media became increasingly consolidated through corporate mergers and less ideologically diverse, and conservatives succeeded in claiming the end of the Cold War as proof that capitalism and democracy were identical and that there is no ideological alternative to the market. The celebration of business, profit, and greed that began in the early 1980s only intensified as the well-being of business was increasingly represented in mass media, popular culture, and news as identical to the health of the nation and the world. In news programs,

CEOs like Louis Gerstner of IBM became the most respected spokespersons about the future of education. The field of education has been greatly remade through corporate influence as business terms of accountability, performance, efficiency, upward mobility, and economic competition have become omnipresent in educational policy rhetoric and journals, displacing traditional discussion of the role of schools in making people who can understand and improve the world or live a full life or participate in civic life. The last chapter elaborates on this transformation and includes discussion of how the latest trends of "performance-based assessment" participate in the corporatizing of public schools.

With the expansion of Edison and other EMOs the teachers' unions have become much more aggressive in countering the company's public relations. Now the American Federation of Teachers, for example, offers on its Web site (AFT.org) not only research on Edison's performance but also information on how to challenge the privatization of public services more generally.

According to Caroline Grannan of San Francisco–based Parents Advocating School Accountability, Edison worked hard to get good news in the press, using in-house public relations and benefiting from the public relations work of local conservative organizations like the California Network of Educational Charters and from the ultra-right think tank Pacific Research Institute. Grannan alleges that at the time that Edison was in danger of being de-listed from Nasdaq following the drastic plunge of the stock price in 2002, it hired a public relations firm specializing in damage control to pump the price of the stock and maintain its listing. Edison hired Harrisburg, Pennsylvania–based Nieman Group to counter a barrage of negative publicity. Nieman's Web site features samples of its print, television, and public relations campaigns for Edison. It proudly includes this quote from *The New York Times*:

> Edison has established a marketing, media and government relations operation that is far more sophisticated and aggressive than those of many corporations, let alone most school systems.

Edison's expansion and survival have involved not only the charisma and sales skills of Chris Whittle and others and the skills involved in repeatedly finding investors to keep the company financially solvent, but also heavy investment in public relations to manufacture positive news. Edison also invested in producing in-house public relations. A LexisNexus search of Edison Schools that includes "Press Releases" turns up nearly as many positive public relations releases from the company as newspaper articles about Edison by journalists. When I met with Grannan in San Francisco in 2003, she indicated that as a career journalist she became involved with the battle over Edison in San Francisco because she believed that Edison was lying about its performance and its financial situation and she thought other reporters were printing Edison's lies without checking them.[50]

FALL

Mark Twain was reputed to have responded to news stories of his passing with the now infamous line, "Reports of my death have been greatly exaggerated." The Edison Schools corporation may not be so lucky.

As of 2002, Edison was in the midst of a whirlwind of interconnected scandals only exceeded by the spectacular collapses of Enron, WorldCom, and Martha Stewart. As the nation's single biggest purveyor of for-profit public schools lost contracts, credibility, and cash, it was singled out by a prominent business magazine as symptomatic of the problem with the U.S. corporation in an article titled, "Why Edison Doesn't Work" while another prominent business magazine gave Edison "An

'F' in Finance."[51] And while the loss of its single biggest contract to date, running sixty of the Philadelphia public schools, looked like its death knell in the middle of May 2002, shortly afterward much-needed cash arrived from investors at least temporarily to plug what looked like a gushing leak in a sinking ship.

Although the Band-Aid cash that Edison needed to start twenty Philadelphia schools was at interest rates more typical of credit cards than business loans, Edison's prospects were brightened by both the Supreme Court's landmark decision that favors public funding of private schools and the partial return of investor capital to the for-profit education sector more generally after a year of radical divestment. While Edison's future is uncertain, what is much clearer is both its troubled past and what is at stake in its survival or demise.

On May 14, 2002, The New York Times ran the headline, "Woes for Company Running Schools." This was a turning point in the national news coverage of the Edison Schools corporation. The New York Times, the Wall Street Journal, and other top readership newspapers had long been reporting favorably on the Edison Schools' bid to become the first profitable privatizer of public schools. The national and local press hailed Edison and Whittle, as a hero for bringing the gifts of the free market to the "failing" public schools of the inner cities. In fact, the Times headline understated the dire situation now facing Edison in the middle of May. Jacques Steinberg of the Times wrote, "The decade long movement to cede failing public schools to private managers, which has usually grown a few schools at a time, achieved critical mass in Philadelphia, when a state panel assigned 42 struggling schools to seven outside operators. The nation's largest for-profit manager of public schools, Edison Schools Inc. picked up 20 of those schools."[52]

Yet now, less than a month later, the national press as well as prominent educational policy experts such as Thomas Toch of the Brookings Institute were lamenting that the possible failure of Edison "would put the [privatization] movement back two decades."[53] Generally glowing news coverage of Edison was transformed to open discussions of the imminent failure of the largest educational management organization and of the notion that Edison was a symptom of the inevitable failure of the educational privatization movement.

Bad press was not the least of Edison's problems.

By May 25, 2002, Edison's stock price had plummeted 94 percent in the past year from well over $20 a share to $1.26. A steady downward slide of investor confidence was fueled by Edison's continued failure to produce profit as well as increasingly dubious prospects for future profitability. Edison's future profitability depended upon increased growth to achieve one-day economies of scale that would allow Edison to operate each school more cheaply than public rivals while turning a profit for investors and outperforming local public schools.[54] The investors needed to see not only that Edison was going to turn a profit one day, but also that it would be able to get more contracts and retain contracts with local school districts by impressing them with a superior school model. At the beginning of 2002, it looked as if Edison was going to exceed the expectations of doubters after the governor of Pennsylvania had seized control of the Philadelphia public schools from the mayor and school board and vowed to turn the entire city district over to Edison.

A public outcry ensued with parents, students, activists, and unions taking to the streets to challenge the plan. Governor Mark Schweiker responded by first abandoning the plan to turn over the Philly schools entirely to Edison and then immediately hiring none other than the Edison Schools corporation to consult exclusively with the state on radical reform for schools. With Edison's input the state concluded that the Philadelphia schools should be taken over by various players, including Edison Schools. While Edison failed to take over an entire city school system — an unprecedented level of privatization — in the end Edison would get twenty of Philadelphia's schools. But the debacle with Philadelphia as well as several other factors would inspire a number of other school districts around the nation to ask some important questions: Were Edison schools worth the money that taxpayers were giving them? Would Edison even be around long enough for the public to know?

The real damage to Edison in Philadelphia was not the loss of its biggest contract to date but the continuing downward spiral of public and private confidence in the company. With the public image unraveling and the stock price down to low single digits, Edison looked to investors either like a really good deal or a money pit. Things looked even worse when, as Edison was losing its big haul controlling the Philadelphia schools, it was forced to announce that it needed to raise $50 million from investors in the next few weeks to cover the cost of starting up the 20 new Philadelphia schools.

Yet more bad press followed when word got out that Edison was talking with Roger Milliken about bailing Edison out for a few months.[55]

Milliken, an 87-year-old textile and chemical mogul, has a history devoted to conservative causes that verges on the radical. The New Republic describes Milliken as "a man who once banned Xerox copiers from his offices because the company sponsored a documentary about civil rights."[56] Milliken's past includes being a top contributor to Pat Buchanan's campaign, membership to the John Birch Society, a reputation for being a virulent union-buster, and "accusations by the Wall Street Journal of holding meetings where participants engaged in 'anti-Mexican banter.'"[57] Milliken was also a major supporter of Newt Gingrich and a funder of a now-defunct private domestic intelligence service called the Western Goals Foundation that was formed to "fill the critical gap caused by the crippling of the FBI, the disabling of the House UnAmerican Activities Committee (HUAC) and the destruction of crucial government files."[58]

Edison's embarrassment of being courted by a notorious right-wing radical with a history of xenophobic statements and ultra-nationalist funding was deepened when a number of newspapers published articles, editorials, and opinion pieces wondering about Edison's business plan depending on "plain old panhandling," as Christopher Byron wrote in an opinion piece on MSNBC. Byron, a former supporter of Edison, notes that the standard criticisms of Edison include its test performance failures and its inability to generate profit. But Byron goes on to say that what has not been adequately recognized is the extent to which the Edison business plan relies on philanthropy and is hence inherently nonmarket based. Elaborating on the charge of "panhandling," Byron writes:

> What else would you call it when a Nasdaq-listed company that is presumably in the business to make a profit, cannot even sell its service to nearly 20 percent of its clients, let alone make any money for itself thereafter, without first soliciting the indirect support of various philanthropic foundations around the country?[59]

And while former supporters such as Byron were explaining Edison's uncertain future for failing to operate truly like a business, others were highlighting precisely the ways that for-profit schooling was rendering public schools unaccountable by subjecting them to the whims of the market. An eighth grader at John B. Stetson Middle School in Philadelphia named Juan Oquendo was quoted in The New York Times voicing fears that his school could simply go out of business: "I look up the Edison stock almost every day. I feel like they're going to take us down."[60]

After an all-night meeting Whittle secured $40 million in financing in the summer of 2002. Of that, $30 million came from the investment firm Chelsea Capital. "Chelsea approached Edison through its general counsel, William B. Wachtel, a New

York lawyer" who "had been friends for 20 years with Benno C. Schmidt Jr., the chairman of Edison."[61] A line of credit for $35 million from Merrill Lynch provided the other $10 million. Carolyn Said, writing in the San Francisco Chronicle noted how expensive the loans were:

> Edison didn't give specifics on interest rates, but said they would be in the low teens — more than double the current national average of 5.35 percent for home equity loans.[62]

To put this in perspective, commercial banks' prime lending rate, which is the benchmark for business and commercial loans, as of May 2002 was at 4.75 percent, a new low since 1965. The loan at least temporarily averted "financial crisis that threatened to derail Edison's expansion into Philadelphia, by far the largest and most ambitious effort in private management of public schools. It also buys time for the company's founder, H. Christopher Whittle, to try to demonstrate that public schools can be operated at a profit."[63] By September 30, 2002, Edison had accumulated $276.3 million in debt dating to 1996 plus $61.8 million in losses prior to 1996.[64]

As it became clear that Edison was desperately scrambling for investment capital in the spring of 2002, the SEC announced that Edison was settling a claim for misrepresenting corporate income to investors. The SEC investigation revealed that Edison had been counting state to teacher payments as company income despite that Edison never received that money. Investors filed multiple lawsuits for misrepresentation of income. According to the SEC, Edison failed to disclose that as much as 41 percent of its revenue consisted of money that it never saw. "In fiscal 2001, $154 million of the $376 million in revenue Edison reported consisted of such district paid employee expenses."[65]

Meanwhile, the Las Vegas, Nevada school district, one of Edison's biggest clients announced that it was refusing to pay

Edison $3 million because Edison had yet to secure $2.2 million that the company had promised the district it would obtain in charitable contributions. Edison promised the school district it would score $4 million in philanthropic funds but only delivered $1.8 million. Walt Ruffles, deputy superintendent of Clark County said, "I think they are so involved in putting Philadelphia together they have us on hold."[66]

To make matters worse, in the same week Edison's flagship school and one of the first Edison schools, Boston Renaissance, announced that it was breaking its contract as of July 2002. The contract had been scheduled to end 2005. The Renaissance School, which had 1,300 students K–8, provided Edison with $9 million revenue annually. But Renaissance was breaking its contract not so much over finances as over performance.

Test results for Renaissance in 2001 show 69 percent of eighth graders failed the state math exam, surpassing the 54 percent failure rate in the Boston school district and the 31 percent statewide failure rate. Other smaller charter schools in Boston far outperformed Edison. The disappointing test performance at Renaissance was symptomatic of larger questions about the Edison model as well as the integrity of score reporting. While multiple independent studies of Edison's test performance found mixed to poor results, scandal surrounded Edison's test performance-reporting practices as well as its testing procedures in the classroom. I take these up in the next chapter.

My contention here is that Edison was not the only one to misrepresent its failures.[67] In fact, the popular press as well as most academic writing about Edison has offered a very narrow view of what was wrong with Edison Schools and why it "failed." In writing that Edison has "failed," I do not mean that the company has gone out of business or that it will inevitably cease to exist. I do mean that it has failed to achieve both its original missions and its financial goals. The original mission of the company was to privatize public schools through voucher schemes. That turned into running public schools through performance contracting. The original curricular model for the company was also nearly completely dropped. Edison also failed as a publicly traded company as the next section details. As well, many analysts believe that Edison will turn increasingly to contracting administrative consulting services, after school, and summer school programs and move farther from both its original mission and even its current activities.

"SOMEWHAT OF A STEAL": THE END OF EDISON AS A PUBLICLY TRADED COMPANY

By the summer of 2003, Edison struck a deal to take the company private again by orchestrating a buyback of its publicly traded stock. First, Leeds Weld, the investment firm headed by former Massachusetts governor William Weld, courted the California Teachers Pension Fund as a purchaser of Edison. From the perspective of many teachers, union members, and pension holders this was an outrageous move on the part of both Leeds Weld and Edison. The proposed deal was not just a matter of selling a risky investment to teachers, thereby imperiling their pensions and risking their financial security after lifetimes of dedication to teaching. It was also a matter of making public school teachers invest in privatization of public schools, which, in the view of many teachers, amounts to an attack on public schools themselves as well as an attack on teachers unions and teaching jobs.

When the 1.5-million-member Service Employees International Union, which opposes public school privatization, learned of the proposed deal in California the members lobbied the California Public Employees' Retirement System against it. Director of the education sector of SEIU Cathy Sarri said, "How can you invest in a firm that will take your dollars and invest in services that will privatize [pensioners'] jobs?"[68]

Not only did Leeds Weld drop its pursuit of the California Pension fund as the buyer of Edison; it then issued a surprising joint statement with SEIU that privatizing public schools is not a viable investment. Jeffrey Leeds announced:

> Investors frequently fail to recognize the political risks posed by investment in companies that pursue privatization of education, and the consequences of long-term financial performance of these companies.... Leeds Weld no longer views companies that pursue privatization of education as likely to generate the long-term growth necessary to offset these risks.[69]

However, a number of publications questioned why the investment firm would be making such a statement as a new deal orchestrated by Leeds Weld was afoot for Edison to be purchased by Liberty Partners, the investment firm handling high-risk investments for the Florida public school teachers' retirement fund. The buyout would mean that Liberty would pay roughly $182 million to own 96.27 percent of Edison and it would control the board of directors of Edison. Whittle would own the other shares and remain CEO.

Despite the announcement against public school privatization, Leeds Weld had profited from the 1999 Initial Public Offering of Edison and it stood to earn "1.95× profit on outstanding Edison warrants if shareholders accept a management buyout offer co-led by Liberty Partners and Edison founder and CEO Chris Whittle."[70] What was going on? Trace Urdan, an education investment analyst at ThinkEquity Partners in San Francisco, viewed the anti-privatization statement by Leeds Weld as a way to deflate the Edison stock price and thereby make the purchase by Liberty Partners go through more easily.

> Leeds Weld will do quite nicely if this [buyout] goes through, and the chances of that happening are aided by folks dumping

on Edison. Some larger shareholders think that the offer is too low, so it helps the deal get done if others are convinced that there isn't an institutional market for the stock, and that shareholders should take what they can get.[71]

The proposed deal for the Florida teachers' pension funds to buy Edison appeared to be moving forward without the input of teachers, public sector employees more generally, teachers' unions, or anyone other than Edison, Liberty Partners, Leeds Weld, and the three pension fund trustees. These trustees responded to protests by declaring that they should not interfere with the deal because that would be "playing politics." The three trustees were politicians: Florida Attorney General Charlie Crist, Florida Chief Financial Officer Tom Gallagher, and the brother of the president of the United States, Florida governor Jeb Bush.

The stock buyback would benefit Edison by no longer subjecting the company's financial dealings to public scrutiny. The secrecy that would come with being privately held would prevent the torrent of public criticisms over finances, stock price, and it would stanch the constant reminder that Edison continues to lose money. Trace Urdan commented:

When they become private, they don't have to tell the public anything. It will be much more difficult for unions and critics to go after things.[72]

The benefits to the key players at Edison would not be small either. In August 2003, Chris Whittle stood to come away from the stock buyback with a $600,000 a year salary plus $4.2 million for his Edison shares and a new loan of $1.69 million despite an outstanding debt to Edison of $10.4 million in loans and interest payments.[73] Of course, the benefit of these favorable loans is that they can generate additional income by serving as investment capital. When the buyback did go through in November 2003, Whittle would do even better for himself.

The proposed deal for the Florida public school teachers' pensions to buy Edison was met with intense public outrage. House Democratic leader Doug Wiles, D-St. Augustine, wrote to Governor Bush:

> Our public employees have dedicated their lives to public service, and I'm certain that the majority would not approve of a significant investment in a business that seeks to eliminate their own jobs.... We must take steps to ensure that the State of Florida is not in the business of bailing out failing private companies.[74]

St. Petersburg High School teacher Don Macneale "felt jabbed":

> "I'm depending on that pension, and so are a whole lot of other people," he said. "To see money invested in an obvious loser like this is outrageous just from a pure financial point of view."[75]

Teachers were not the only ones who considered the purchase a bad investment.

> There is no disputing that investors have a low opinion of Edison Schools. The company went public four years ago for $18 a share and peaked at $36.75 a share in 2001. Last year it traded for as little as 15 cents. Thursday it closed at $1.68, just a little below the buyout price of $1.76 a share.[76]

Although Urdan describes Edison as "somewhat of a steal" for losing unprofitable contracts and shifting the business toward summer school contracting and software licensing, he is in the minority of investors. Of 72 potential investors contacted by Bear Stearns on behalf of Edison, only 19 met with Edison and four "expressed serious interest."[77]

If analyst Urdan thought that the deal was "somewhat of a steal" for investors, the critics thought it was somewhat of a "steal" for different reasons. Reg Weaver, the president of the National Education Association wrote to Governor Jeb Bush, pleading with him to stop the deal:

It seems to me that given Edison's poor performance, sizable debt, and limited future prospects, the retirement savings of Florida's public education employees may be at risk. It is my understanding that Edison was $73 million in debt as of September 12, 2003, according to the company's SEC filings. Edison's share price has dropped from over $36 in February 2001, to less than $2 a share today, a decline that cost the company's shareholders millions in shareholder value. I question why this investment was chosen when other more promising investments might well have been available.[78]

Weaver's letter, which appeared in the press on September 30, 2003, highlighted the National Education Association policy, which states:

The Association believes that the assets of retirement systems in which public education employees participate should be managed and invested for the sole and exclusive benefit of the participants and beneficiaries of those systems.... Trustees should consider, among other items, opposing investments in corporations whose policies or expenditures of funds undermine child welfare and/or public education, when other investments provide equivalent benefits to retirement systems boards.[79]

Governor Bush did not respond by halting the deal. Instead, he responded that he did not know about the deal and should not know about the deal.[80] The *Palm Beach Post* came out with an editorial on October 9, 2003 describing the deal as a "double stinker": "The politics smells and, more to the point, so does the bottom line."[81] The paper stated that although the governor should not be responsible for watching every deal done on behalf of the pension fund, if an investment is an "obvious stinker," then the governor has an obligation to act. Refuting the claim from Bush that interference would be politicizing the investment, the paper drew a comparison between the trustees' questionable past investment in Enron and the pending investment in Edison.

> Governor Bush and the other trustees, Attorney General Charlie Crist, and Chief Financial Officer Tom Gallagher, say they won't interfere with the deal, which will be final next month if Edison stockholders approve. The Enron debacle of two years ago should be a lesson. The state pension fund lost $325 million when Alliance Capital kept buying Enron even as it skidded to death. Alliance's managing partner also sat on Enron's board. "Interference" then wouldn't have been political; it would have been smart. In any case it's hard to claim that the pension fund has no political dimension. The administrator is Coleman Stipanovich, brother of lobbyist and former Jeb Bush staffer John "Mac" Stipanovich.... The state should ensure that there is no insider entanglement like the one that tainted the Enron fiasco. The state should explain how the deal makes financial sense. Certainly it does for Mr. Whittle, who gets a bundle for his stock and a salary increase to $600,000.[82]

What the paper did not go on to mention is the close ties between Enron and the administration of George W. Bush (brother of the Florida governor) nor more pertinently the relationship between Edison and members of the administration of George H. W. Bush (father of the Florida governor). An angry constituent of Jeb Bush named Stephen M. Hodges wrote the

Tallahassee Democrat newspaper on October 13. His letter highlights the broader issue of school funding that can often be obscured when the debate shifts to the best methods of privately investing public resources.

> It is outrageous that Gov. Jeb Bush and the Florida Cabinet are going to spend $182 million from the state's pension fund to bail out a failing private business: Edison Schools. Created by the same brilliant visionary who introduced TV commercials in public school classrooms, Edison has been kicked out of two-thirds of the districts it has contracted with. The typical Edison school performed below average, and Edison has never — until this year — shown a profit. [Author note: This claim of profit by Edison has been called into question because it was made at the time that debt went unreported.] ... No wonder it's not attracting investment dollars! The real kicker here is that the governor is planning this while scheming to overturn a clear public mandate to properly fund our public schools. Our schools are dead last among the 50 states in high school graduation rates. If you're digging yourself a deeper hole, the first thing you must do is stop digging. Put the shovel down now, Jeb, and properly fund our public school system.[83]

Jeb Bush's willingness to put Florida teachers' pension funds into privatizing public schools should be understood in relation to his efforts to resist a democratically mandated small class size initiative in Florida. There was a citizens' initiative voted in during the 2002 election mandating smaller classroom size. Bush was against it, vowed to punish Floridians for voting for it, balked at it, and tried to get it put back on the ballot and revoted. He said it was impossible. However, by Florida law, he needed to adhere to democratically approved citizens' initiatives, and there was a specified date when this had to be accomplished. One of the solutions was to graduate students earlier, thus thrusting the whole problem onto the college system, which is also vitally underfunded in Florida. Another solution might have had to do with pushing some kids into charter schools like Edison. The class-size amendment was a big deal in Florida and the governor's resistance to it was daily big news.

On November 12, 2003, active and retired union workers covered by the Florida Retirement System went to New York to protest the buyback deal outside of the Edison shareholders meeting. Ralliers represented the American Federation of State, County, and Municipal Employees (AFSCME), American Federation of Teachers (AFT), Florida Education Association (FEA), National Education Association (NEA), Service Employees International Union (SEIU), and the Teamsters. Not only did protesters decry the lack of employee representatives on the Florida State Board of Administration that administers the pension plan, but they also pointed out that the FSBA lost more than $428 million in Enron and WorldCom. Protesters also railed about the dubious track record of Liberty Partners.

> An analysis of Liberty by an outside consultant hired by the State of Florida (and obtained through a Freedom of Information Act request) raised troubling questions about Liberty's judgment and performance. The analysis found that, although Liberty has produced a higher return than the S&P 500, most of the excess return has been the result of just two investments and that without those investments, Liberty's returns would have "substantially underperformed" the S&P 500.[84]

The protests did not stop the deal. Edison shareholders approved the purchase, the trustees did not intervene, and Edison was purchased by Liberty.

In the end Chris Whittle came out of the deal with about $21 million dollars, a 42 percent raise, a loan of $1.68 million, and eligibility for a bonus of 245 percent of his base salary.

One of the most incredible aspects to the end of Edison as a publicly traded company is that future low performance of the for-profit company hurts public school teachers. While public teachers' money is tied up in Edison, they cannot get detailed information on the financial workings of the company that they own. What is more, criticisms of this for-profit business principally hurt public school teachers by imperiling their retirement funds.

The buyback scheme should be understood as a continuation of Chris Whittle's use of the public sector to accumulate private profit. From Channel One, to the public purchase of the Whittle Communications campus, to the original plan for Edison, to the pension fund buyback, Whittle has profited and helped other wealthy investors profit by taking advantage of the public sector and public schools.

In the chapters that follow I further recount the history of Edison Schools that includes but surpasses questions of whether Edison was efficiently run as business. I also do not settle with the question of whether for-profit schools operate efficaciously and compete with public schools for efficient delivery of education. These concerns that dominate both popular press and academic discussions about Edison and privatization make assumptions that liberals and conservatives share, namely, that everyone agrees on the role of schooling.

Increasingly public schooling is almost exclusively discussed largely for its role in offering individual students knowledge and skills for economic opportunities in the economy and for the national role of making workers for the economy so that the nation can compete in the global economy. I assume here that the primary roles of public schooling should involve helping students acquire knowledge and skills that allow and even encourage them to be participants in democracy. That is, I view the potential of public schooling as doing more than offering students such capacities as functional literacy, functional numeracy, or cultural literacy.

Rather, public schooling ideally also offers students tools for understanding and criticizing unequal power relations as they are produced and reproduced throughout various places in society. In this critical perspective, knowledge, culture, and curricula are always studied with an eye to how they affirm or contest relations of domination and subordination in society. Democratic schooling in this case is not merely about the school taking on a "democratic" format with such reforms as challenging traditional hierarchical classroom format. Nor is it merely about including all students in lessons and curricula. It also involves linking what goes on in school to questions of ethics, politics, and power in society, and it highlights the extent to which knowledge is implicated in making a more or less just world. As distinct from the primarily economic basis for discussing school privatization that dominates popular press and academic discussions, my discussion here is principally guided by the political and ethical roles that schooling can take. Consequently, my discussion will return repeatedly to a more basic question of American education. That is, what is the role of public schooling in a democratic society and how do for-profit education companies such as Edison fit into schooling for democracy? The next chapter examines Edison's model and curriculum with regard to these concerns.

2

BUT DOES IT WORK?

Edison sells its program to school districts and parents by promising an innovative school design. Although the Edison school design is "traditional" (as opposed to various progressive models), the features that the company promotes as its biggest advantages are better academic achievement measured by tests, a longer school day than the public school standard, a strong emphasis on technology, a curriculum backed by "scientific research," an emphasis on testing and management of student progress, and a highly structured and disciplined environment. Edison also promises exceedingly motivated and professional teachers whose motivation comes, in part, from the financial bonuses they can earn if students achieve high test scores.

There are some important questions to ask of Edison's model. The first is whether it is more effective than non-Edison schools. Do Edison's innovations work? Do kids learn more at Edison schools? This might seem like a pretty straightforward question. Edison claims that they can establish the superiority of their model with test scores and that this is really the conclusive way to measure success. Critics, armed with a number of studies, conclude that Edison has not raised scores. But lurking behind this seemingly simple question about effectiveness are several other tricky questions: What are public schools for? How do we decide what is important for students to learn? Who should decide what is important for students to learn? Is there only one "right" way to teach history, English, math, science, and languages, or are there different ways to teach these subjects with radically different implications depending on one's guiding beliefs about the purpose of school?

The goals of this chapter are (1) to consider some of what makes Edison's model distinctive, (2) to examine its innovations and effectiveness, and finally (3) to look at some of the broader issues just mentioned including the beliefs that underlie the organization of the school and its curriculum. This third goal shifts the frame of the debate about effectiveness that dominates the popular and academic conversation about Edison.

The vast majority of academic and popular press discussion of Edison has focused on test performance and financial aspects of the company. The two questions most asked about Edison by liberals and conservatives are whether it works to raise test scores and whether it works financially to decrease costs. Asking whether or not something "works" brackets out of consideration the broader goals, purposes, and underlying assumptions about what something works to do. The focus on test performance and finances has thoroughly eclipsed discussion of whether Edison facilitates democratic education and a democratic society. If one assumes that the democratic potential of public schools should be at the forefront of debate, then the question of whether or not Edison "works" may be the wrong way to approach the company and public schooling more generally. Before discussing the problems with this approach to evaluating Edison I address what makes their model distinct from public schools, including test performance, technology, the longer school day, Edison's widely adopted Success for All reading curriculum, and its widely adopted Everyday Mathematics curriculum.

EDISON'S PERFORMANCE

According to Edison, its schools and students show improvements greater than the improvement of average public school students. According to a wide range of studies and critics including scholars, politicians, teachers' unions, students, parents, and activists, Edison's claims are untrue, creatively manipulated, and inaccurately reported.

I believe that readers should be skeptical of over-reliance on standardized tests as the measure of educational quality although I realize that not everyone will be so willing to turn to the vast array of alternative measures for assessing educational quality. (This is worth a book in itself and a number of good recent books take up these issues.)[1] Assuming one accepts the social value of standardized tests, how does Edison fare? Measures of Edison by a number of organizations offer a picture of performance that does not live up to Edison's promises to improve significantly student performance on math and reading tests.

Two major studies of performance have been conducted. One was done by the Evaluation Center at the University of Western Michigan (2000) with funds from the National Education Association and another was conducted by the American Federation of Teachers (AFT). These studies have been sharply critical of Edison's self-evaluations. Edison in turn dismisses these studies as necessarily biased because they were conducted by or with funding from teachers' unions. Edison is paying for a study by the Rand Corporation, which it suggests will be impartial. That report was to be released in 2004. Although that study was not reported as this book goes to press, a major finding of inferior test performance by charter schools in comparison to public schools made national headline in Fall 2004.[2] Every study has particular assumptions framing it as well as particular methodologies for interpreting the data. This is not to say that an impartial study of Edison's performance is impossible. However, the results and methodological approaches to Edison performance are hotly disputed. In part, in the case of Edison, this is because there is little clear, decisive, and conclusive evidence for test score improvement across Edison's schools or in relation to schools in the same districts.

The authors of the Western Michigan University (WMU) Evaluation Center study conclude, "Edison students do not perform as well as Edison claims in its annual reports on student performance." In summing up their study they write:

> When seeking new contracts, Edison promises districts and charter school groups that its model is a successful one. In this report, we examined the question of whether Edison did more in terms of student performance on standardized achievement tests. We selected schools that have a long record to trace, and we looked at a variety of test results with its first 10 schools. While our findings do not suggest that Edison did less, they do not suggest that the company did more with these schools in terms of gains on standardized tests.[3]

Edison Chief Education Officer John Chubb responded angrily to the WMU study. In a press release he was quoted as saying:

> Despite the mountains of statistics designed to give it an aura of legitimacy, the study is a political attack piece, pure and simple. It is shocking that social scientists would attempt to pass off such work as an objective evaluation.[4]

Chubb, a social scientist himself, has been one of the leading advocates of privatizing public schools. Having written numerous articles, book chapters, and books on the subject, he claims neutrality while being highly paid by Edison Schools and linked to pro-privatization think tanks (Hoover Institution, Brookings Institution).

A more serious point Chubb makes is that Edison schools' test scores in the study were compared with "less disadvantaged" schools in the district. Chubb stated, "Edison is asked to manage some of the lowest-performing schools in the nation. In these schools it is important to evaluate the progress they are making, not how they compare with schools that are already successful."[5] However, the authors of the study rebut Chubb's charges:

> Edison claims that we do not take into account that its students are more disadvantaged than the comparison groups we used. In comparison to statewide or national averages, students at Edison schools can certainly be characterized as "disadvantaged," as Edison claims. However, the characteristics of the students in its schools are generally similar or less disadvantaged than students in the districts in which they reside.... When comparing the student characteristics in the 10 schools in our study with the local districts, we found that, if anything, Edison students were less disadvantaged.[6]

Although there are a number of other disputes over the meanings of the test scores and the studies, it is worth noticing how Chubb frames Edison as stepping in to help "disadvantaged" students without either addressing how it is that those students became "disadvantaged" or addressing how Edison aims to target the most "disadvantaged" schools for profit.

The AFT report found similar conclusions to the WMU study. In 2000, the AFT study updated an earlier study conducted in 1998 that compared achievement data from states in which Edison operates schools to data provided by the Edison Schools corporation. The study found, "Students in Edison schools mostly perform as well as or worse than students in comparable schools; occasionally they perform better."[7]

John Chubb called the report "a political diatribe dressed up in the guise of science."[8] The AFT updated the report again in 2003 and concluded, "averaged across all states, the typical Edison school performed below average."[9]

Resembling corporate quarterly progress reports, Edison treats student assessment as one of its ten fundamentals of the curriculum design. These assessments release student test reporting data on four areas of evaluation: (1) state and district tests; (2) benchmark assessments; (3) structured portfolios; (4) quarterly learning contracts.

According to Edison in annual company reports, public relations press releases that are widely picked up by the media, conferences, and workshops, students are making large and substantial improvements in measurable "achievement gains."

In the 2000–2001 school year, Edison widely reported that 84 percent of its schools achieved "positive gains." However, Edison's School Performance Report lists 62 schools that it reported as making "positive gains" in a year in which the company claims to have run 113 schools. As Caroline Grannan of San Francisco-based Parents Advocating School Accountability pointed out, 62 of 113 schools is 54.8 percent rather than the 84 percent claimed by Edison. Grannan writes that a closer look reveals that 10 of the schools that Edison lists as making "positive gains" have had their contracts dropped; although Edison was no longer running the schools, the company still reported them as part of the success story. Further, 10 of those schools that Edison lists as positive are considered by their states as "failing schools":

Among failing Edison Schools that the corporation has listed as successes are Edison-Henderson Academy in Dallas, Texas; Boston Renaissance Charter School in Boston, Massachusetts; Edison-Bethune Charter Academy in Fresno, California; Edison-

McNair Academy in Ravenswood School District, East Palo Alto, California; Phillips-Edison Partnership School in Napa, California; Seven Hills Charter School in Worchester, Massachusetts.[10]

The findings of the studies were enough at odds with Edison's claims about its performance that U.S. Congressional Representative Chaka Fattah (D., Pa.) called on the investigative arm of Congress, the General Accounting Office, to open an investigation of Edison.

A TEST: ONE QUESTION, MULTIPLE CHOICE, UNTIMED

1. In the spring of 2001 Edison Charter Academy made headlines when it came in last in test scores among all San Francisco elementary schools. It made headlines not for having such bad scores but because it spurred the San Francisco United School District to revoke Edison's charter. Guess how Edison rated the performance of this school.

(A)"Positive" (B) "Positive" (C) "Positive"
(D) "Positive" (E) All of the Above

STOP. Pencils down.

Answer: E

If making up a test in which all of the answers are the same seems like cheating, then it would be in the spirit of how Edison has been accused of administering its tests.

In addition to charges that Edison manipulated test reporting, it has been accused of encouraging cheating on tests in classrooms. This scandal erupted in the winter of 2002 when the

Wichita Eagle reported that, in interviews with seven former Edison teachers, four of the seven said that they had been told by the company "to do whatever it took to make sure students succeeded on standardized tests, including ignoring time limits, reading questions from a reading comprehension test aloud and in some cases correcting answers during a test."[11]

Three of the seven former teachers claim to have told the company about testing irregularities although Edison denied being warned. Teachers claimed that testing rules were ignored on state and district assessments as well as the national MAT–7. Ingalls-Edison elementary administrators were fired when an investigation revealed that time limits were ignored and questions read aloud on the MAT–7. One teacher who reported irregularities to Edison witnessed another teacher correcting answers on students' tests. Another teacher who did an exit interview with Edison reported to the newspaper, "I looked like a piece of scum because my kids didn't do well, but that was only because I didn't cheat."[12] Another teacher who explained that cheating took many forms stated, "You had to do what you had to do just short of doing the test for them."[13]

The scandal prompted the board of the *Wichita Eagle* to issue a strongly worded call for further investigation of Edison and a denunciation for Edison's failure to investigate, thereby forcing local authorities to do so. The newspaper, which had formerly written favorably of Edison, was now calling for breaking the contract with the company should charges be confirmed.

> We don't tolerate cheating by students. We don't tolerate cheating by principals. And should the charges prove true, we must not tolerate cheating by Edison. (For the board, Phillip Brownlee)[14]

Shortly thereafter, Wichita broke contracts on two of its four Edison schools. The Wichita community's reports of its experiences with Edison differ markedly from the reports Edison offered in its Fourth Annual Report on School Performance, September 2001, page 17. Edison wrote:

> In many of Edison's partnerships, such as Wichita and Mount Clemens, communities are as proud of the widespread gains that Edison schools seem to have helped stimulate as they are of the gains in the Edison schools themselves.

According to educational psychologist Gerald Bracey of George Mason University, the glaring disparity between what went on in Wichita and how Edison represented it was not an isolated case but rather part of a pattern of Edison repeatedly misrepresenting the public about the academic performance of its schools.

AN EMPHASIS ON TECHNOLOGY

> In the classroom, technology enhances students' productivity, efficiency, creative expression, communication, and access to information.... Every member of the Edison national system is electronically connected via The Common, Edison's intranet message, conferencing, and information system. Connecting to The Common allows members to communicate with one another and also to tap into the vast electronic resources that Edison makes available.
>
> — From the Edison Web site

Technology, according to Whittle's original dream, was to be a major distinguishing element of the Edison schools. However, early experiences with giving laptop computers to every child were extremely expensive disasters. Children and families were not given proper instruction in how or why to use the computers or how to set them up, not to mention instructed on proper care and maintenance. In fact, Whittle himself points out that the amount of money spent on computers is about equal to the massive amount of debt that Edison has incurred. Edison largely abandoned this component of its plan, thereby making Edison less distinct in its model from other public schools.

Despite what Edison may have suggested to parents or teachers, the early plans for extensive use of technology appear interwoven with Whittle's courting of major investors in the tech sector. In the spring of 1991, *The New York Times* reported the following:

> If the blueprint is successfully completed, Mr. Whittle said he intended to build 200 schools that he expected would initially enroll 150,000 students from 3 months to 6 years of age. The students would eventually be able to complete high school at these schools. The cost to open them, Mr. Whittle estimates, will approach $2.5 billion to $3 billion, much of which he thinks he will raise by selling stakes to three or four large companies that supply products to schools. Although he would not mention any names, logical candidates to invest might be a computer maker like IBM or Apple, which might try to sell their machines to schools.[15]

Whittle's interest in technology may have concerned more than its capacity as a teaching aid and as a way to convince computer companies to invest in the Edison Project. In 1992, people familiar with Whittle's background were skeptical about underlying motives for the Edison Project.

> Critics charge that Whittle is merely looking for an avenue to inject commercialism into schools. They envision school halls lined with billboards.[16]

Critics may have been naïve about the commercial potential that the advertising ideaman may have seen in wiring for-profit schools. Whittle repeatedly courted major media corporations

— including Paramount, Viacom, Disney, and Time Warner — that might be able to profit by not only running schools for profit but also by advertising their products and other products to students in those schools through multiple media.

> Every kid in the late 1990s, Whittle says, will carry a lightweight portable "unit" — some futuristic interactive laptop allowing him to access information networks and teaching programs and multimedia "texts," allowing teachers to administer and grade tests, allowing parents to look in on homework and such. Whittle and his financial partners could also make a lot of money selling it.[17]

Whether or not the Edison Project was initially viewed as a way to generate profit through technology sales or possibly to extend school commercialism to place advertising into schools through these "digital lunchboxes," it is clear that technology was central to the corporate school vision of Whittle and others.

Today the wild drive for "computer literacy" for teachers and students, the emphasis on instructional technology, and the general faith in technology as an inherently educative and liberating force belie another yet more disturbing faith — a (radically misguided) faith in the corporation to provide employment, fair work conditions, security, and a general state of bounty for the student, for the nation, and for the world.

While few argue against sufficient school technology such as computers and software, a question arises: if these are important components of a well-resourced public school, then why not make these a universal publicly provided resource in schools? Private companies such as Edison are not necessary in order for access to technology to be expanded from the best-funded schools to all schools. When the private sector becomes involved in public schooling, profit-taking is a guaranteed component. For example, the educational publishing companies sell public schools a number of computer programs. Whatever one thinks of the quality of the software programs and accompanying teacher training, the companies charge school districts thousands of dollars per classroom per year for these programs. Sometimes as much as half the cost of a teacher's salary for a year! If the public schools use publicly developed and publicly owned versions of, for example, an early literacy program, the cost is guaranteed to be radically less per student, per classroom, and per school. As I discuss in Chapters Three and Five, the No Child Left Behind legislation championed by the George W. Bush Administration is designed to profit financially educational publishing and software companies that will receive federally mandated remediation contracts. Reform legislation could have instead funded the development of inexpensive publicly owned and freely distributed programs for public schools without draining public tax coffers to enrich companies like Pearson NCS, McGraw-Hill, and Scholastic.

Providing laptops was one of the ways Edison initially sought to entice parents. In doing so, Edison was appealing to the popular idea that future employment prospects for students are increased by familiarity with computer hardware and software. Corporate CEOs such as Louis Gerstner of IBM and Junk Bond felon and education entrepreneur Michael Milken emphasize that in order for the United States to compete successfully in global markets, it needs a highly trained and "computer-literate" workforce. Of course, computer skills such as word processing or databases and the Internet are useful tools for anyone. However, with the exception of those working in computer-related fields, the vast majority of the workforce, especially those who use computers for work every day, have need for no more than basic knowledge of computer technology. The way students and teachers use technology in the classroom is very different from the promises it holds as a symbol of progress, development, and efficiency. Alex Molnar explains:

Although clichés about the "computer literacy" needed to navigate the "information superhighway" are used with great authority by corporate executives, politicians, and educators, there is no commonly agreed upon definition of either term. No one knows what "computer literate" students would know or be able to do, much less whether it would be desirable for them to do it. And no one can describe what a school in the fast lane of the "information superhighway" looks like or how its revolutionary new design can be reasonably thought to increase student knowledge.[18]

Likewise, educational theorist and technology historian Douglas Noble reminds us that corporate attempts to "revolutionize" American education with technology have been going on since the 1960s; yet the vision of the brave new world of the high tech school has changed almost yearly:

1983: Teachers are told to teach students how to program in BASIC.

1984: Teachers are told to teach LOGO to help students think as well as program.

1986: Programs of individualized instruction promise to "lead to the world of tomorrow."

1988: Teach Word Processing!

1990: Curriculum-specific computer tools such as history databases become the next big thing.

1992: Students are supposed to learn to program hypertext multimedia.

1994: The Internet is it!

1995: Censoring and limiting student availability to the Internet is it.

1996: Every student should have a laptop computer.

2000: Computer reading programs will overcome illiteracy.

2003: Homeschooling and charter schooling will be transported into cyberspace to become "virtual classrooms."

Edison's corporate education dream of networking students to teachers and teachers to administrators in New York, to managing attendance, test scores, and curriculum progress, to digitalizing the last bit of what goes on in the classroom — it did not work to make Edison profitable or to make Edison superior to other public schools. What has become increasingly clear to educational researchers, however, is that what does work is distinctly low-tech solutions such as small class sizes, small schools, low student–teacher ratios, human interaction, and approaches to learning that begin by taking seriously what students find meaningful and relevant to their experiences.

This is not to devalue the worth of computers as tools. However, computers are just that — tools. They do not replace critical thinking skills such as the ability to question and investigate. Nor does "computer literacy" necessarily help students to develop what some educators refer to as "critical literacy," which is an ability to understand how social, political, historical forces work to create the world students find themselves in. Critical literacy is especially important for nonwhite working-class and poor youth (those whom Edison targets) because youth with greater critical literacy have a stronger sense of possibility to challenge and transform stifling and oppressive conditions rather than merely adapt to them.[19]

A LONGER SCHOOL DAY

According to the company, Edison Schools, the K–2 school day is an hour longer than normal and the 3–12 school day is two hours longer. On its Web site, Edison claims that its longer school year of 198 days "makes more sense for families today." Edison contends that more hours in school means more learning.

This may be true. However, if Edison is in fact performing lower or roughly equal to the public school average as the studies by the University of Western Michigan and the American Federation of Teachers suggest, it raises a number of serious questions about the ideal of the longer school day. What does it say about Edison's quality if its schools are working teachers and kids harder and getting lower or even similar results? Might kids be better off attending schools that do not require more time for the same results and that allow them extra time with their families or communities? Are non-unionized teachers being overworked at Edison schools?

Considering that the parents Edison targets are working longer and longer hours for less money,[20] it would seem that Edison is really offering childcare services to parents whose increasing work time decreases time with their families as income declines. This raises the question of whether a lack of adequate public funding for childcare services is being turned into an investment opportunity for wealthy investors.

To complicate matters, as French Sociologist Pierre Bourdieu established nearly three decades ago,[21] and as a number of contemporary scholars affirm, schools tend to reward and bolster the knowledge attained by middle-class children in the family and other middle-class milieus while punishing and denigrating the knowledge learned by working-class and poor children in their families and in other working-class milieus. That is, schools tend to reward the attainment of knowledge and speech that expresses the interests and concerns of the most powerful groups (this knowledge of privilege Raymond Williams calls the "selective tradition"[22]) while simultaneously misrepresenting this knowledge as accessible to all. Put yet another way, the most powerful groups in society monopolize the production and distribution of select knowledge deemed of most value while mechanisms such as testing and tracking make this knowledge appear as equally attainable and as unrelated to the interests of different classes and racial and ethnic groups. Testing and tracking in schools appear to make student access to this knowledge a matter of individual hard work, merit, and intelligence. In fact, access to this knowledge comes principally through the home and the social and cultural milieu. Bourdieu's research suggests that equalizing schooling cannot result from attempts to expand access to middle-class knowledge whether by extending the school year or by other remediation attempts. What may be in order to foster democratic education is not remediation efforts to enforce knowledge that is misrepresented as objective, neutral and value-free but rather reinventing the educational process so that teaching and learning focus specifically on the ways knowledge relates to different and competing social values, groups, and power interests. Learning, in this sense, is not just about learning to assimilate to the currently existing social order, but about learning to remake society in more democratic, equal, free, and just ways. To put it bluntly, a longer school day presumes that educational opportunities come from students learning more of what schools offer. However, if schools actively reproduce and replicate social hierarchies and inequalities, then it is necessary to rethink the role and function of schools rather than merely try to give kids more schooling. There is a long, progressive legacy of scholarship and school design and practice that aims to transform schooling in more democratic ways from John Dewey, George Counts, Paulo Freire, Michael Apple, Henry Giroux, Donaldo Macedo, Lilia Bartolome, Peter McLaren, Antonia Darder, Ira Shor, The Rethinking Schools collective, and many others. There are also many public schools and public school teachers across the country already teaching critically. The discussion below of the Edison reading and math curriculum explores through concrete examples the difference between Edison's approach to learning and democratic approaches.

THE EDISON CURRICULUM: STRUCTURED OR RIGID?

Edison claims to provide curriculum that includes reading, math, history/social studies, science, writing, and world languages as core subjects (when I visited Edison Charter Academy I learned that it does not teach foreign languages although it has a large number of non-native-English-speaking students and does not offer bilingual education either). It also has classes in character and ethics, physical fitness and health, music, dance, visual art, drama, and "practical arts and skills" offered at various levels. Edison reports four methodological approaches to instruction in the classroom: project-based learning, direct instruction, cooperative learning, and differentiated learning.[23]

Edison promotes its curriculum as benefiting not only from employing multiple teaching methods but also from being highly structured. As a public fight was brewing over Edison taking on a major management role in the Philadelphia public schools (see Chapter Four), an article appeared in The New York Times on February 17, 2002. It described an Edison School in Flint, Michigan.

> Based on a typical day at the Garfield Edison Partnership School here, Philadelphians can expect 90 minutes of reading lessons each morning, during which teachers follow a common script; swift disciplinary hearings for students who so much as talk out of turn in class; standardized tests administered by computer every few weeks, with answers transmitted instantly to Edison headquarters in New York; and, eventually, a complimentary computer in the home of every child. Parents should also get accustomed to their children receiving law-enforcement-style tickets — but for good conduct — which are the currency for admission to school activities like the honors choir and Friday night dances.[24]

If this sounds like an overload of discipline for students, many former Edison teachers have described conditions in Edison schools that squelch teacher creativity and student intellectual curiosity.

> "I remember visiting the school that first year and thinking, 'I could never work here,'" says school board member Mary Hernandez, an Edison supporter. "I told Edison, 'You've got to let them have a life.' And sure, there were all the pressures and stress of a start-up, but it didn't get better the second year."... Staff also chafed at the rigid culture of Edison. "I think a lot of people felt like they were corporate clones, all having to teach the same thing at the same time," says Caceres. "People questioned the uniformity of it all. Maybe that works in Texas, or Colorado. But this is San Francisco, and people are used to being able to question, to be themselves."... "We feel like we were disposable teachers," one departing Edison teacher told the *San Francisco Bay Guardian*, the muckraking local weekly that has covered the school and its problems intensively. "They think that they can just plug anybody in — any human thing with a pulse — train them, and that's it."[25]

Teachers' experience of rigidity is unlikely to be alleviated by either Edison's reading or math curriculum, Success for All and Everyday Mathematics.

SUCCESS FOR ALL?

Success for All is what many teachers referred to as a "canned" curriculum. That is, despite claims to the contrary by its designers and advocates, it is a highly scripted program that leaves little in the lessons up to teacher control. Most discussion of Success for All in academic debates has focused on its efficacy. That is, nearly all of the heated and sometimes data-laden discussion has concerned whether or not Success for All raises reading test scores.

The most vocal of its defenders is its developer and tireless promoter Johns Hopkins education professor Robert Slavin. Slavin contends that Success for All is a proven success. Slavin co-edited a book on Success for All that largely frames the program as a success. However, as Patrick Groff writes, even Success for All supporters have doubts:

> SFA [Success for All] advocates Steven Ross and Lana Smith reveal in their chapter in the book, called "Success for All in Memphis," ... that although their tests of the effectiveness of the use of SFA in "high-poverty schools" were "suggestive of positive program effects," the "results can hardly be considered conclusive that SFA will raise reading performance in every grade in every [such] school" (p. 72).[26]

Groff offers an excellent review of scholarship that to different degrees finds negative results of Success for All. He is worth quoting at length on this literature.

> It may be, as they [Slavin and Madden] presume, that SFA's successes constitute "the most promising approach [at present] to scale-up federal, state, and other support to help establish and maintain professional development networks like ours." However, there is notable dissension as to SFA's exclusive entitlement to that honor. For example, Bobbie Greenlee and Darlene Bruner find "more favorable results [on literacy development] are being achieved in non-SFA Title 1 [low-income] schools." Steven Ross and Lana Smith discover "no favorable differences" on "standardized achievement tests" for second-graders given SFA instruction. Ross, Smith, and Jason Casey also report that in only half of the school districts they examined was there evidence "generally supportive of SFA benefits for all students." ...Other detractors of SFA are even more emphatic in their criticism of it. Stanley Pogrow, for example,

believes that "the inescapable conclusion remains that research carried out by SFA supporters, at least in America, finds success, while school districts and independent research reports are entirely negative" about its effectiveness. Herbert Walberg and Rebecca Greenberg agree that "numerous independent reviewers have found essentially negative evidence" about SFA. They add that those who favor SFA "did not have the time to locate and study the negative evaluations of SFA." Therefore, they go on, implementing SFA "is worse than doing nothing because it wastes money, conceals the problem, and impedes productive solutions."[27]

One of the most persistent and vociferous critics of Success for All is Stanley Pogrow, a former New York City public school teacher and professor of education at the University of Arizona. As Pogrow argues, what is at stake in whether or not Success for All actually delivers on what it promises is more than this particular reading program but rather the powerful influence that its developers have had over the course of educational reform across the nation. Recall the New American Schools (NAS) group that began under Bush, Sr. Pogrow points out, "This is now a lobbying and fundraising group that promotes seven models of comprehensive school reform, the largest of which is SFA."[28] Pogrow reveals that not only Edison but a small number of others with ties to NAS, such as Allan Odden of University of Wisconsin, promoted the wide-scale use of Success for All without evidence of its success. According to Success for All founder Robert Slavin:

The loan from the New American Schools Investment Fund came at a time when no one else would give us a loan. We had assets of zero dollars and zero cents. We could not have gotten a loan from a bank and we couldn't use foundation grants because it wasn't enough money. So, the loan was critical as a bridge to move us out of our parent organization and establish the Success for All Foundation. I don't know how else we could have done it.[29]

According to the NAS Web site:

NAS is a non-partisan, non-profit education organization that provides educators with comprehensive strategies for school reform, improvement, and assessment. It was founded to encourage education reform by a group of CEOs from large corporations in 1991, many of whom sit on its board of directors today.[30]

Pogrow points to a number of studies that demonstrate not only that Success for All has not resulted in improvement in reading, but also that it may be responsible for declines in reading scores in multiple places where it was implemented. According to Pogrow, wide-scale use of Success for All in Baltimore, Miami-Dade County, Florida, Columbus and Cincinnati, Ohio, in Mississippi, Memphis, Tennessee, San Antonio, Texas, among other locations showed declines or a lack of improvement relative to improvements made in the area. Pogrow highlights "a large and consistent set of independent studies" to bolster his case against the claims made by Success for All. Pogrow and other critics of Success for All should be taken very seriously. Readers should look at these studies and reports to see whom they want to believe about the efficacy of Success for All on reading tests. However, my principal concern here is not with the controversy over the scores and the issue of efficacy but rather with the extent to which Success for All contributes to a broader social climate that fails to make schools that help students and teachers to question and understand the world in ways that might lead to their participating in society and changing it for the better — to make it more democratic, equal, and just.

As useful as Pogrow's criticisms of Success for All are, they do not challenge the "whatever works" mentality that has become nearly all-encompassing with regard to school reform. The "whatever works" mentality, as part of the broader common sense that looks on schooling as preparation for competition in the workforce, presumes that one learns to read to be able to function in society, to fit into the economy. For example, although Groff criticizes the results of Success for All, he attributes this to Success for All being a too "indirect, nonintensive, and unsystematic manner of teaching phonics information." One big problem with this view of reading programs for efficacy is that implicit in them is an understanding of reading as a functional skill apart from reading as what Paulo Freire referred to as the practice of freedom. Freire wrote of reading the word to read the world to change the world. Freire's thinking provides contemporary progressive critics of Success for All a very different criticism of Edison's reading program than the ones argued over by Pogrow, Slavin, and other educational researchers.

There are two main progressive criticisms of Edison's curriculum and organization. The first concerns the teaching methods and school styles that Edison and other EMOs embrace. This criticism points to the rigidity of the Edison approach: standardized curriculum, standardized delivery times, heavy testing, rigid classroom discipline, centralized control over what goes on in classrooms, phonics-based reading instruction, scripted lessons, long school days, long school years. Critics such as Alfie Kohn, Gerald Bracey, Harold Berlak, and others suggest that part of the danger of corporations such as Edison running schools involves the threat posed to such progressive educational methods as Whole Language literacy instruction, love of learning for its own sake, "a penchant for asking challenging questions, or a commitment to democratic participation in decision making

uplift. In Kohn's view, the classroom ought to model democracy for students. Consequently, the classroom should be a place that fosters free exchange of ideas, encourages curiosity and doubt, eschews competition, and imbues students with a sense of the inherent value of other people, cultures, and the unknown.

Another progressive critic, Henry Giroux, in his book *Teachers as Intellectuals*,[33] advocates schools that are places where teachers' pedagogical decisions can be guided by their intellectual projects and their visions for how these projects contribute to the making of a more just, equal, and free society. In Giroux's perspective the teacher is not a deliverer of information that others devised. Instead, teachers begin with students' experiences and help students understand those experiences in terms of broader social, historical, cultural, political, and ethical questions. As what Giroux calls a "transformative intellectual," the teacher has the potential to engage with students in a process of understanding how knowledge relates to power, how knowledge is made by people rather than merely inherited, how knowledge expresses particular groups' interests. For the teacher who is a transformative intellectual, the focus on understanding knowledge in relation to power is part of envisioning the educational process as a means for social change. In Giroux's perspective, consequently, decisions about what to teach and what not to teach, how to frame issues and questions, are not merely technical pedagogical questions. They are also political questions in that they frame the past and present in ways that always affirm or contest relations of oppression and domination. As well, such questions need to be continually questioned, interrogated, and rethought with changing contexts.

Both Kohn's ideal of the classroom as model for democratic society and Giroux's ideal of the teacher as a transformative intellectual are profoundly different from the corporate visions put forth by Edison's Success for All reading curriculum employed in primary and elementary schools. Common to both

Kohn's and Giroux's and many other progressive educators' ideals of democratic schooling is the importance of teacher autonomy, relating the curriculum to the broader social concerns, issues, and problems that inform the daily lived experiences of students, and understanding that students are motivated by knowledge that matters to them.

Contemporary economic and political realities point to a major flaw in the way that education is discussed in newspapers, on TV, by politicians, the Department of Education, and a great number of educational experts. This minimalist view of schooling as making workers for the economy, education as a consumable commodity, education as a chance of individual upward mobility — none of these takes into account what the progressive American philosopher John Dewey described as the need for democratic education.

> [The democratic] test of all the institutions of adult life is their effect in furthering continued education.... Democracy has many meanings, but if it has moral meanings, it is found in resolving that the supreme test of all political institutions and industrial arrangements shall be the contribution they make to the all-around growth of every member of society.[34]

First, consider the following description of the Success for All reading program taken from its Web site. Then, look at the sample of reading instruction that the same site provides:

> **Success for All** is a comprehensive restructuring program for elementary schools, based on the following principles:
>
> - Emphasis on prevention, early and intensive intervention, and tutoring for students with academic difficulties.
> - Incorporation of state-of-the-art curriculum and instructional methods.

- Emphasis on the integration of phonics and meaning-focused instruction, cooperative learning, and curriculum-based assessments.
- Writing/language arts instruction emphasizing writer's workshops.
- Pre-school/kindergarten instruction with story telling and language development.
- Adaptations for Spanish and English as a second language.
- A family support program engaging parents, community members, and integrated services.
- Extensive professional development throughout the elementary grades.

Despite the avowal of having "state-of-the-art curriculum" and meaning-focused instruction, one typical example of a Success for All lesson that the company provides on their Web site paints a starkly different picture. As I elaborate following the example, it also illustrates a curriculum thoroughly at odds with the progressive democratic ideals discussed above. This lesson excerpt is reprinted with permission from the teacher's guide available on the Success for All Web site:

DAY 1

Story Summary: Kitaq (git-AWK), a young Eskimo boy who lives with his family in a small seaside village in Alaska, wants very much for his grandfather to take him on his first fishing trip. Can Kitaq walk all the way to the ice-fishing holes and back without getting too cold and tired? Grandfather takes Kitaq fishing and is proud when Kitaq catches his first fish. After a successful, but tiring day of fishing, Kitaq rides part way home on the sled. Kitaq's family celebrates his first catch by inviting friends and relatives for a feast that Kitaq helped provide.

EXTENDED STaR

Story Preview

Display and discuss the book's cover. Encourage the children to tell what they think is happening. Share the title of the story, *Kitaq Goes Ice Fishing*, with the children and have them predict what the story will be about. Highlight at least 2–3 illustrations from the story that convey story meaning, yet do not tell the entire story. Using previewed illustrations, encourage the children to make oral predictions of what they think will happen to Kitaq. Record several predictions on the chalkboard or on chart paper.

The lesson continues with a "Predictive Student Writing Activity" for a journal entry.

The children may be given a predictive sentence starter like: I predict that Kitaq will ...; I think the story will be about ...

The next day the teacher is supposed to introduce the story by referencing the predictions from the day before.

Present any vocabulary that is central to the understanding of the story. Explain how difficult the journey will be in the ice and snow if Kitaq goes ice fishing. Point out Alaska on a map or globe. Invite the children to tell about their own fishing experiences. List reasons why Kitaq may not be able to go ice fishing with his grandfather, Apa. Compare the type of fishing in this story to that in *Let's Go Fishing*.

The teacher reads the story interrupting to ask questions such as:

Page 1: **Was Kitaq older or younger than his brothers?** *[Kitaq was younger since he did not go to school yet, like his older siblings.]*
Page 3: **Why did Kitaq get up early on this particular morning?**

What did Father say Kitaq would have to be able to do before Grandfather would take him fishing?

Page 7: **What do you think Kitaq was thinking about while he was waiting for Apa to eat his breakfast?**

Page 10: **Why didn't Kitaq go to school with his brothers and sisters?**

Page 16: **Do you think Kitaq will catch any fish?**

Page 20: **How do you think you would feel if you were sitting beside Kitaq? Why did Grandfather say they must stop fishing and start for home now?** [*They needed to leave for home before it got dark so that they would not get too cold or get lost.*]

The next day the teacher keeps at this and then encourages students to recall aspects of the story like title, characters, setting, problem, and solution. Students are encouraged to retell the story in a number of ways:

Interactive Story Circle: The students take turns elaborating on the details and ideas expressed by the last participant without repeating the sequence, but instead try to add to the sequence of events to complete the story.

Sequence Cards: There may be occasions when story-sequencing material can be used to foster the group retelling of the story.

Story Dramatization: The students share the sequence of the story through dramatization. Many stories lend themselves to dramatization.

Sharing: The teacher and the children share their favorite story events with one another.

Story Maps: The children organize the story structures to convey the sequence (or path) of the story and the pattern of the story.

On the third day the teacher is supposed to prompt students to answer "higher-order" questions:

> Why did Kitaq want to go ice fishing with Apa?
> How do you think Kitaq felt on the long trip home?
> Why was Apa proud? How do you know?
> Do you think Kitaq was old enough to go ice fishing?
> Why or why not?
> Do you think Kitaq will want to go ice fishing again?
> How do you know?
> How do you think you would feel about ice fishing?

Students are taught to judge the story as though making a newspaper movie review with such methods as "Thumbs Up/Thumbs Down," rating the story by awarding it stars, and explaining what they liked or did not like.

> *Story Rating:* Assist the children in developing a story-rating system. As a class, evaluate the story according to the rating criteria. For example:
>
> 1 star = engaging title
> 1 star = enjoyable characters
> 1 star = eye-catching illustrations
> 1 star = interesting story
>
> *Story Critique Frames:* Encourage the children to tell what they either liked or disliked about the story.
>
> I liked the story _____ because _____.

Students are asked to explain why they would recommend or not recommend the story. An "individual story conference form" for the teacher gives the teacher questions to ask students:

Questions for Individual Story Retelling

1. Recall the name of the story. *[Kitaq Goes Ice Fishing]*
2. Recall the characters. *[Kitaq, Apa, Aana, Aata, two brothers, two sisters]*
3. What did Kitaq want very much to do? *[Kitaq wanted very much to go with Grandfather for his first fishing trip.]*
4. What did Kitaq need to do before he could go on his fishing trip? *[Kitaq needed to be able to walk to the ice-fishing holes and back without crying when his feet got cold and tired.]*
5. What happened when Kitaq began to fish? *[Kitaq felt a bite on the line and he pulled out a large, silvery pike fish.]*
6. Why was Kitaq happy about the fish he caught? *[Kitaq was happy because he could feed his whole family with the fish he caught.]*
7. How did Kitaq's grandfather feel as he pulled Kitaq home on the sled? *[Kitaq's grandfather felt proud of Kitaq for catching his first fish.]*
8. Why would Kitaq's mother prepare a feast? *[Kitaq's mother would prepare a feast so that family and friends would learn that Kitaq was old enough to fish and help feed his family.]*
9. What was your favorite part of the story? Why?

This is only an excerpt from one Success for All lesson. However, it readily illustrates a number of dire problems with the curriculum from the vantage point of democratic education. These problems concern both the content of the lesson and the methodology of Success for All.

This lesson, ostensibly "multicultural" and concerned with questions of cultural difference, addresses culture, difference, and social relationships in many ways that are antithetical to the kinds of democratic ideals suggested above by Kohn, Giroux, and Freire.

In his teaching handbook Steven Jacobson paints a very different picture of Yup'ik life, culture, and history. It is erroneous to regard today's Yup'ik culture as explicable solely in terms of the culture that existed here before Europeans arrived, just as one cannot explain today's general American culture solely in the light of pre-revolutionary colonial culture. In fact, Yup'ik culture has been more drastically influenced by outsiders during the past century than has general American culture. Missionaries successfully persuaded Yup'iks to give up their own religion in favor of Christianity by claiming that the latter was a universally appropriate religion. They had at least as much, if not more, effect on Yup'ik culture as did the school authorities (for whom they set the stage) who sometimes successfully and sometimes unsuccessfully urged Natives to give up their own languages in favor of English, claiming the latter was a universally appropriate language for Americans.[35]

At issue here is not only the extent to which the SFA curriculum misrepresents culture, drawing instead stereotypical caricatures while aiming to appear "culturally sensitive." Also at issue is the ways that the curriculum designers elected to focus on particular activities of the characters that treat cultural difference as a touristic novelty rather than as interwoven with historical power struggles. For example, the meaning of being Yup'ik that is presented by the story is one of family bonding by enduring the natural elements, for boys learning to fish, and for girls learning to cook. The depiction paints a fictitious primitive culture that is outside of modern technology as well as outside of the real daily struggles faced by native Alaskan people who contend with racism, the theft of their native land, the cultural and economic impositions of the state and federal governments, as well as multiple problems brought on by commercialism including diabetes from a diet that does not consist wholly of freshly caught fish. Within the view of this lesson, the history of first Russian and then U.S. imperial conquest and demands for cultural assimilation in part by Christian missionaries are not merely absent; they are actively erased. Also erased is the relationship between actual cultural difference and the realities of work. Are native Alaskan males fishing for sustenance while females await their return in igloos? Do native Alaskans have the same work opportunities and educational opportunities as the majority white residents of Alaska?

> Modern houses with electricity have replaced the qasgiq and enet. Small towns with churches and schools have replaced the traditional winter communities, and airplanes supply the residents with modern supplies. While many residents fish and trap for a living, the economy of the communities is also dependent on public monies in the form of wages and salaries to government-employed workers, creating a situation of dependence on government rather than the traditional practice of self-sufficiency.[36]

While the Success for All story *Kitaq Goes Ice Fishing* emphasizes education in a family, that is, going fishing with grandfather, it makes no reference to the history of education that the Yup'ik endured including the destruction of their language and culture largely through schooling that was justified on the basis that "Children must be kept in school until they acquire what is termed a common-school education, also practical knowledge of some useful trade." and on the basis of "reclaiming the Natives from improvident habits and in transforming them into ambitious and self-helpful citizens" as "Education continued to reflect the philosophy that Natives should be assimilated into the white culture."[37]

It is utterly essential to consider the implications of this strategic erasure of history and reality from a curriculum about a historically oppressed group, the Yup'ik, that is being taught principally to other historically oppressed groups in the Edison schools — that is, to working-class and poor African Americans and Hispanics. Why should these students *care* about the story or the questions? From the perspective of the advocates of Success for All and other "enforcement-oriented" curricula, the test scores and extrinsic rewards of gaining the "knowledge" are the basis for the motivation. Just as the Yup'ik had their language and culture assaulted on the basis of making them into "ambitious and self-helpful citizens" by learning trades, so, too, largely African American and Hispanic working-class students in Edison schools find their cultures and languages assaulted on the promise of upward economic mobility.

To return to the question of motivation from the perspective of the progressive tradition, knowledge should be meaningful to students. For working-class and poor students of color who know oppression firsthand, the plight of native Alaskans would directly relate to their own experiences of having their language devalued, of having their culture erased and denigrated as a pathology by the culture of power,[38] of having their history defined through colonial and imperial violence.

There are a number of ways that a story about native Alaskans and what they do and how they live could be made meaningful, relevant, critical, and fascinating for students. But the Success for All curriculum fails to begin with the knowledge and experiences of the students in any particular classroom and community. Ideally, these experiences and knowledge would be linked to the newly introduced curriculum. Furthermore, the role of the teacher in helping students to discover knowledge that is meaningful, to help students deepen an understanding of why this knowledge might matter to them, to raise questions about whose version and perspective of knowledge is expressed and why — all of these key critical interventions are not only absent from the Success for All curriculum, but they are vigorously prohibited by the rigid structuring of time and the various ways that teachers are forced to stick to the curriculum. The Success for All methodology presumes that teacher autonomy in the classroom can only be a deficit.

Success for All needs to be recognized as a highly politicized curriculum not only for the kind of knowledge it propagates as universally valuable, but also for the prohibition on the pursuit of critical questions about curriculum that it demands. The above lesson could easily be made critical in the way I have taken it up.

A predictable response to my criticism would be that I want to politicize an apolitical curriculum and raise critical questions about power with children who are too young to comprehend such issues. However, it is imperative to recognize the profoundly political nature of the Success for All curriculum itself. For students who have firsthand experience of oppression, as the majority of the Edison students do, questions of power in relation to culture, language, and work are not foreign but omnipresent in daily life. Furthermore, it is necessary to reject the idea that the Success for All curriculum simply delivers neutral knowledge and skills. Curricular designers make particular decisions about what to include and what to exclude, what stories to tell and whose stories to tell and how to represent situations. These again are political decisions in part in that they affirm or contest dominant understandings of the world that maintain or transform its present unjust state.

While at present too little of public school education is structured to encourage critical education, there are public school teachers who do teach critically as I illustrate in the next section dealing with the limitations of Edison's widely used mathematics curriculum.

Free progressive curriculum is widely available from such places as the Rethinking Schools Web site and its links. Many practical books, journals, magazines, and Web sites on teaching for social transformation rather than merely economic assimilation can be adopted by individual teachers and school administrators as well as school boards. Web sites include National Coalition of Education Activists, schoolcommercialism.org, Corporate Watch, Fairness and Accuracy in Reporting, The Nation, ZNET, In These Times, New Internationalist, The Progressive, Dollars and Sense, Gay Lesbian and Straight Education Network, Adbusters Media Foundation, Center for Economic Conversion, Inequality.org, Harpers.org. Books by bell hooks, Ira Shor, Lilia Bartolome, Donaldo Macedo, Jonathon Kozol, Bill Bigelow, Linda Darling-Hammond, James Loewen, Ira Shor, Pepi Leistyna, Robin Truth Goodman, Howard Zinn, Robin D. G. Kelley, Antonia Darder, Noam Chomsky, Eduardo Galleano, Robert Moses, Bill Ayers, to name just a few, offer clear, well-written material that links education, learning, and knowledge to many aspects of social justice. However, in privatized schools with corporate curriculum, the possibility of teaching for a more just, critical, and democratic society is prohibited not only through rigid curriculum but also by the fact that criticisms of the role of the corporate sector in threatening democracy are off-limits.

EVERYDAY MATHEMATICS

Edison uses Everyday Mathematics in the primary and elementary schools. According to Edison's Web site:

> The curriculum stresses computation and a full range of mathematics including data collection and analysis, probability and statistics, geometry, and prealgebra. To teach math at this level we use the University of Chicago School Mathematics Project's Everyday Mathematics, a research based program proven to raise achievement levels.

Like Success for All, Everyday Mathematics is embroiled in controversy. Proponents of Everyday Mathematics see a program that is attentive to making math meaningful for students by relating the subject to what students know and care about. Critics suggest that this attention to math in context compromises students' mastery of mechanical operations like memorizing times tables. Both sides of the debate remain within the question of the efficacy of the math program.

There is a difference between functional numeracy and critical numeracy. Arguments for functional numeracy suggest that schools should teach students math so that they will have skills for work and consumption in the future. It is toward these practical and vocational concerns that Everyday Mathematics aims. Some even suggest that the pleasure of mathematics knowledge is both valuable in itself and that it provides students with entry into another way of thinking about the world. Along these lines, critical numeracy suggests that math learning should relate math to what students find meaningful and, hence, motivating; in addition it suggests that this knowledge can be the basis for understanding how power is wielded in society and can form the basis for empowering students to be more active and participatory citizens. Let us look at two ways of teaching about the relationship between fractions and percentages. First, consider the Everyday Mathematics approach. Unit 9 of Everyday Mathematics for the fourth grade teaches about fractions and percentages. The fourth grade Assessment Handbook of Everyday Mathematics offers some examples of activities:

Making a Percent Booklet (Lesson 9.1)
Writing and Solving "Percent-of" Number Stories (Lesson 9.2)
Solving Challenging Discount Number Stories (Lesson 9.4)
Graphing Survey Results (Lesson 9.6)
Ranking Countries and Coloring a Map to Show Literacy Data (Lesson 9.7)
Writing and Solving Division Number Stories with Decimals (Lesson 9.9)
Find the "Fraction-of" and "Percent-of" a Design (Lesson 9.10)

The following concrete example of learning about fractions is taken from the link provided on the Everyday Mathematics Web site to the Everyday Mathematics Resource Guide from Kent, Washington.[39]

The lesson, titled, "MARS FRACTION HUNT," was written by Paul T. Williams of the Vanguard Honors Program in Phoenix, Arizona. It is designed for grades three to five. According to its author, "This lesson is designed to give the students practice in the use of fractions, changing fractions, using equivalent fractions, and paying attention to detail." The stated objectives include helping the student learn to divide a word into fractional parts, "use equivalent fractions to correctly divide words," pay attention to detailed instructions, and analyze clues and decode a message.

> RESOURCES/MATERIALS NEEDED: A MARS candy bar, classroom globe (on a small stand or cradle), activities paper. Before the activity, the MARS bar should be hidden under the classroom globe. The ANSWER KEY for the activity is: FOR THE FIRST ONE TO FINISH THIS THERE WAITS A PRIZE IF YOU USE YOUR HEAD. CLUE MARS IS DIRECTLY BENEATH THE SOUTH POLE. GO LOOK.

For "Activities" the lesson explains, "The student will write the appropriate parts of the words on the line to form a new word. When the message is complete, the first student to decode the message will be rewarded by finding the hidden candy bar (MARS bar)." In a section titled "Tying it all together" the lesson explains, "After the winner has claimed "his prize" the students review the assignment. The author of the lesson writes:

> During this exercise, many of the students claim that "no such words exist." This is where it is necessary for them to pay

attention to the details of the instructions. Usually the brighter students will be the ones to win; in that case, the teacher could team the students into pairs or small teams — if this is done, it is best to be sure to have a MARS bar available for each winning team member.

Recall from above, Paulo Freire's democratic ideal of learning to read the word in order to read (understand) the world in order to change the world. While the Mars bar lesson begins with an object that is familiar and interesting to some students, a candy bar, the point of the lesson is to learn to divide words to learn discrete skills and ultimately to get loot. In this lesson, learning about fractions and percents becomes part of a puzzle game that reduces mathematics to a practice of consumption. As well, intelligence in this example is defined as cleverness in the pursuit of extrinsic rewards and intelligence is not linked to ethical concerns. There is a politics to this math pedagogy. In this case learning math skills is ultimately for the acquisition of external rewards. In class this external reward takes the form of a candy bar. But later, if students can master enough skills, the rewards of consumption can be greater and greater.

Compare the above list of lesson ideas and the elaborated sample lesson with two lessons from a math teacher in Chicago. Both lessons are relevant to students' lives, but the lesson that follows is critical. The teacher, Eric Gutstein, did not use Everyday Mathematics:

Driving While Black/Driving While Brown — DWB/DWB
A Mathematics Project About Racial Profiling

This is a group project ... one packet to be turned in for the group, with everyone's name on it, *except* for the *Individual Writeup* at the end which everyone must do separately.

In this project, you will investigate the issue of racial profiling, which is also sarcastically called Driving While Black (or) Driving While Brown (DWB/DWB). African Americans and Latinos *all* over the United States have complained, filed suit, and organized against what they believe are racist police practices — being stopped, searched, harassed, and arrested only because they "fit" a racial profile — that is, they are African American (Black) or Latino (Brown). But is this true? How do we know? And can mathematics be a useful tool in helping us answer this question?

Part I. Review some basic probability ("chance") ideas. With your partner or in your group, please work through the attached pages from Take a Chance. You can write directly on the sheets and you do not need to write out any explanations. These activities are just supposed to help you review and get back into thinking about probability and chance.

Part II. Finding the percentages of African American, Latinos, Whites, and Asians/Native Americans in Chicago. In the envelope you have a number of small cubes (DO NOT LOOK!!). These cubes are color coded: tan is for White people, yellow for Asians/Native Americans, red for Latinos, and black for African Americans. The percentages of each of the cubes (approximately) matches (or simulates) the percentage of those people in Chicago. For example, if everyone in Chicago was Latino, there would be nothing but red cubes in your envelope. Your job is to figure out what percentage of Chicago's population is White, Latino, etc. but you can ONLY pick *randomly* a SINGLE cube, RECORD its color, and REPLACE it in the envelope. So you will be conducting an experiment (picking and replacing 100 times in total), collecting data (recording each pick), and analyzing data (determining from your picks, how many of each color there are, that is, determining what are the racial/ethnic percents in Chicago).

Use the charts on the next page to record your picks. Use tally marks for each pick, and then record the results of every 10 picks in the table. Make sure you record the fraction and percentage of each race/ethnicity for every 10 picks in the table as well.

1. What do you think is in the envelope? WHY???
2. What happened as you picked more times and what do you think would happen if you picked 1,000 times?

PART III. Investigating DWB/DWB. Here are some data from Illinois, based on field reports filed from 1987–1997 (this is only a small sampling of the data). In an area of about 1,000,000 motorists, approximately 28,000 were Latinos. Over a certain period of time, state police made random 14,750 stops for no apparent reason. Of these, 3,100 were Latino drivers. Using what you learned in Part II, set up your own simulation of this situation. First you will have to find what percentage of the motorists were Latino, then you will have to find what percentage of the stops were of Latino drivers. Then you will have to use the cubes you have (you can combine them in your group if you need to) to set up a simulation of the random traffic stops. Record your data, carefully, and see if you do 100 random traffic stops (that is, picking, recording, and replacing), what percentage of the time do you pick a Latino driver.

3. What percentage of the motorists in part III were Latino?
4. What percentage of the random traffic stops were Latino?
5. How did you set up the simulation for problem #3 (that is, how many "Latino" cubes, how many total cubes do you have)?

6. What was the result of your 100 picks, that is, how many Latinos were picked and what percentage is that?
7. Do your results from #6, based on your simulation experiment, support the claim of racial profiling? Why or why not?
8. INDIVIDUAL WRITEUP (answer all four questions, please ... and use extra paper as needed!)

What did you learn from this activity? How did you use mathematics to help you do this? Do you think racial profiling is a problem, and if so, what do you think should be done about it? What questions does this project raise in your mind?

PROJECT: FLORIDA TOMATO PICKERS TAKE ON GROWERS

Instructions: In this project you will read a newspaper article (which we will go over in class) and answer several questions. This explains how you are to hand in your final report. READ THESE DIRECTIONS VERY CAREFULLY!!! You have one week, so ASK IF YOU HAVE QUESTIONS!!!!

PROBLEMS TO SOLVE:

1. In the article, Sr. Rocillo says that he made 45 cents for each bucket of tomatoes. What is the percent increase or decrease from 1981 to now for what he makes per bucket? (Make sure you say whether it's an increase or decrease!)
2. The pickers are asking for an increase in their pay to 60 cents a bucket. What percent increase are they asking from their current *average* pay per bucket?
3. The pickers say they make an average of $9,000 a year.

   a. Based on that figure and based on the average pay for a bucket, about how many buckets would someone have to pick in a year to make that much money?
   b. How many pounds of tomatoes would that be?

4. The article states that the picking season is from September until May. Using your answer to #3b above, and other information in the article, give an estimate of how many pounds of tomatoes someone would have to pick:

   a. in a day,
   b. in an hour, and
   c. in a minute

   to make $9,000 in a year. Make sure you explain exactly what your assumptions are in making your estimate (for example, how many days worked in a month, how many hours in a day, etc.).

   Then, the next time you are in a grocery store, use a scale and figure out how many tomatoes are in a pound, then say how many tomatoes you would have to pick to make that money in (d) a day, (e) an hour, (f) a minute.

5. According to the Florida Fruit and Vegetable Association (the Growers), tomato pickers in Florida make more than $16,000 a year. However, the Coalition of Immokalee Workers, who represents the tomato pickers, claims the growers overestimate the hours the pickers really work, and that the pickers make only $9,000.

   a. How much more percent do the Growers claim the pickers make than the Coalition claims?
   b. Based on your answer to #4 above, how many hours a year does the average picker work?
   c. And based on the answer to #5b and on the Coalition's estimate of the average annual pay for a picker, what is his or her average hourly pay rate?
   d. The federal minimum wage is $5.15 per hour. Is your finding for the average hourly pay rate of the tomato pickers more or less than minimum wage? By how much percent is it more or less?

6. In our last unit, Cereal Numbers, we studied the Consumer Price Index (CPI). Make a graph that has two pieces of information on it ...

7. [EACH PERSON MUST ANSWER #7 INDIVIDUALLY, IN FULL PARAGRAPH FORM!] According to the article, "... it is estimated that 40% of agricultural workers [mostly Haitian, Mexican, and Guatemalan immigrants] are in the United States illegally and are thus easier to exploit."

   a. What does that mean? What does exploit mean? Do you believe that the tomato pickers are exploited? Why or why not, and if so, by whom?
   b. In the last paragraph of the article, Sr. Rocillo says that he is staying put and plans to work "as long as the body takes it." What would you do about this whole situation if you lived in Immokalee, trying to support your family on what you earned picking tomatoes? Why would you do this?

Both the Mars bar treasure hunt lesson showcased on the Everyday Mathematics link and the DWB/DWB investigation and Tomato Pickers lesson share an aim of motivating students by making Mathematics meaningful. As well, they share an attempt at integrating math with language learning. However, there are a number of glaring differences in how the lessons make math meaningful and how they relate student knowledge and experience to the study of math.

The deficiencies with the Everyday Mathematics approach to math are readily apparent when contrasted to Gutstein's DWB and tomato pickers lessons. Gutstein's lessons begin with social problems that affect students and their community and then asks students to use the math skills to determine whether the problem is real, to determine how bad the problem is, to analyze the veracity of the claims made about the problem by different interests. It then uses the skill to relate the problem to other problems or broader configurations of power. In this way the lessons begin with what is meaningful to students but then helps students relate the meaningful knowledge to democratic concerns with equality, freedom, justice, and power sharing, and it helps students consider how individuals or communities can act with the new knowledge to transform the situation. It is essential that teachers understand the implications of the authority they wield in the classroom and connect their actions to the broader implications they have outside the classroom. Is a teacher principally an agent for making loyal consumers and disciplined workers who have mastered basic skills ready for use by employers and advertisers? Or is a teacher principally an agent for making future citizens capable of understanding the world and how it is shaped by power to be able to act with others for the benefit of all?

Everyday Mathematics does not necessarily have to be turned into lessons in consumerism as in the Mars bar lesson. In fact, the Mars bar lesson could be modified to address meaningful social problems, issues, and conflicts related to, for example, consumerism, marketing to youth, public health, work conditions and ownership from cocoa bean picking in West Africa to checkout counter in Kent, Washington. The fact is, however, that there will be limits in a for-profit school like Edison regarding how these methods can be employed. These are different visions guiding public-oriented versus corporate-oriented practice. The central question is: Can an Edison school, a privatized public school with vested interests in a corporate-dominated economy and culture, allow democratic approaches to learning math and reading that at the very minimum engage with the politics of the curriculum by investigating how knowledge relates to power? Can a corporate school allow democratic approaches to knowledge that question and even challenge corporate visions of social control and instead propose public visions of democratic control? Institutions do not commit suicide.

To offer an analogy in mass media, the June 2003 Federal Communications Commission's deregulation that allowed even fewer massive media companies to buy more of the nation's television, radio, and newspaper — an issue that according to Michael Kopps of the FCC would dramatically affect all Americans by further homogenizing the content of the media and eliminating local control — was scarcely covered in corporate media, which essentially wrote the new legislation for conservatives politicians to implement. Because most Americans rely on corporate news from the same companies benefiting from the new legislation, most citizens had no idea about what was being done until just before the ruling when it was almost too late to stop it.

Content is affected by who controls the media. "Five media conglomerates — Viacom, Disney, Time Warner, News Corp, and NBC/GE — control the big four networks (70% of the prime time television market share), most cable channels, vast holdings in radio, publishing, movie studios, music, internet, and other business sectors."[40] This has much to do with why there are no programs in corporate media that explore the kinds of questions about power raised by Gutstein's math lessons. These sorts of questions can typically be found to a limited extent only on public television on programs such as Bill Moyer's "NOW" or on a public radio program like Gretchen Helfredge's "Odyssey." Public institutions allow questions and deliberation about the public interest to be raised, in part because they are less limited by profit motive and the interests of advertisers.[41] Public schools are some of the only public institutions where this can be done in depth. While currently and historically public schools have not fostered the kinds of questioning, deliberation, and debates about matters of public import, there are a number of teachers and public schools that do foster such a democratic culture. While public democratic culture needs to be expanded in public school, it is certain that privatizing and corporatizing public schools will do just the opposite by limiting the ways that curriculum such as Success for All and Everyday Mathematics can be used to develop public democratic pedagogies to address pressing matters for students in schools targeted by Edison. As these examples illustrate, the control over teachers' time and the content of the curriculum are deeply political issues. Current reform initiatives like high stakes tests, standardized curriculum, and scripted lessons aim to remove teacher control over time and content and hence ensure that particular questions are not raised in schools.

BUT DOES THE EDISON PROMISE OF ECONOMIC OPPORTUNITY WORK?

In the Introduction I wrote that while Edison does not promise to solve the problems of poverty and unemployment that plague some communities, it does promise to offer something close: educational opportunities for students who may be able to cash in their knowledge for good jobs. Is this a credible promise?

Between 1980 and 1997 the U.S. economy created 32 million new jobs. Most of these jobs were in the service sector. At the same time 1.6 million manufacturing jobs disappeared despite the fact that manufacturing output increased dramatically by more than 66 percent. Another 2.6 million manufacturing jobs were lost during the George W. Bush administration.

> Factory work has never been fun, but it once offered secure and relatively well paying jobs to men and women who were willing to work hard. Not any more. Many have lost their jobs due to downsizing and plant closings. The drive to make U.S. manufacturing lean and mean has worked. Workers are so much more productive now that firms can make do with fewer of them. While some service-sector jobs pay well, they often fail to match the pay and benefits of traditional factory jobs. Relatively unskilled work such as data entry, scanning groceries,

and telemarketing pays poorly, offers few benefits, and often is limited to part-time hours. In 1997 the average hourly compensation was $13.17 for a manufacturing job and $11.58 for a service job.[42]

Despite the economic boom of the 1990s, real wages have steadily declined since the 1970s and wealth has become increasingly concentrated at the very top of the economy. These facts point to a problem with Edison's corporate model. That is, if Edison creates schools on the model of corporate culture, what does it mean that most Edison students cannot be participants in the part of the corporation that continues to benefit — namely, the management part. In reality, most Edison students who will be able to find work at all will be participants in the other corporate culture, the service labor part. This is a reality of decreasing wages and benefits and fewer unions to represent workers' interests. It will take civic participation, political participation including labor and rights organizing to assure that future workers enjoy the standard of living they deserve.

These realities point to a major flaw in the way that education is discussed in newspapers, on TV, by politicians, the Department of Education, and a great number of educational experts. This minimalist view of schooling as making workers for the economy, education as a consumable commodity, education as a chance of individual upward mobility — none of these take into account either the real economic conditions and limits of the present system or the role of education in preparing citizens for civic and political participation.

WHY "WHATEVER WORKS" DOES NOT WORK

Sometimes it makes sense to ignore the broader purposes and goals of whether something works. For example, when we brush our teeth in the morning we do not need to examine every morning the purposes of scrubbing our choppers, weighing and considering the pros and cons of dental hygiene versus dental neglect. However, sometimes ignoring the broader purposes and goals of whether something works can have grave moral or political consequences. Adolph Eichmann, the architect of the Nazi killing machinery of Auschwitz woke up in the morning, put on his coat and hat, went to work, sat down at his desk, designed mass execution methods, went home, had dinner with the family, perhaps listened to some music, read some poetry or a novel, and went to bed. To ask whether or not Eichmann's designs for mass human slaughter were effective, of course, cannot be separated from the implications of what he designed. Likewise, the implications of our school designs cannot be treated like brushing our teeth. U.S. public schooling affects millions of children, teaching them not just facts or information but also ways of thinking about others and the world. If the United States is to have a democratic future with an educated citizenry capable of performing not just functional or salable skills but also the promise of self-governance and the capacity to treat other citizens and nations humanely, then lively public debate over the meaning of these goals must ensue. The Eichmann example is a little too easy. If we are to take seriously the ideal of a self-reflective citizenry and nation, we ought to ask how our current approach to school practice and school reform addresses our own practices at home and abroad, not merely those of a government toppled more than half a century ago.

For example, how might we understand schooling in relation to the facts that despite its status as the richest country on the planet, the United States is failing its most vulnerable citizens with the highest rates of child poverty in the industrialized world; the nation's capital has child poverty rates as high as forty-five percent.[43] Henry Giroux writes in *The Abandoned Generation* that a "war on youth" is being waged in the U.S.:

[T]he hard currency of human suffering as it impacts on children can also be seen in some of the astounding statistics that suggest a profound moral and political contradiction at the heart of the United States, of one of the richest democracies in the world: 20 percent of children are poor during the first 3 years of life and over 13.3 million live in poverty; 9.2 million children lack health insurance; millions lack affordable child care and decent early childhood education; in many states, more money is being spent on prison construction than on education; and the infant mortality rate in the United States is the highest of any industrialized nation. When broken down along racial categories, the figures become even more deplorable. For example, "In 1998, 36 percent of black and 34 percent of Hispanic children lived in poverty, compared with 14 percent of white children."...While the United States ranks first in military technology, military exports, defense expenditures, and the number of millionaires and billionaires, it is ranked eighteenth in the gap between rich and poor children, twelfth in the percent of children in poverty, and twenty-third in infant mortality. One of the most shameful figures on youth, reported by Jennifer Egan in the New York Times, is that "1.4 million children are homeless in America for a time in any given year ... and these children make up 40 percent of the nation's homeless population." In short, economically, politically, and culturally, the situation of youth in the United States is intolerable and unforgivable.[44]

The war on youth described by Giroux is symptomatic of a broader turn away from public services and public priorities and services as health care, social security, Medicare, Medicaid, and what is left of welfare, all subject to calls for defunding and privatization. A troubling course has been charted, and not only on the domestic front.

The philosopher Theodor Adorno wrote that after Auschwitz the value of education must be viewed in relation to the need to avert future vast atrocities. Millions of people, many Auschwitzs of people, die every year unnecessarily as a result of both neglect and policies designed to enrich very few people while circumventing global democratic governance. Meanwhile, entire school curricula are organized in ways that avoid crucial recognition of how the world is governed in ways that allow this to happen. Civics lessons teach abstract principles of democracy while seldom addressing how power is wielded in Washington through corporate lobbies; history classes seldom teach about the economic and material interests underlying historical conflicts; economics classes in high school teach about supply and demand and free trade while generally avoiding the matter of how international financial organizations and powerful states determine who benefits and who loses from such policies; meanwhile, science and math are all too often taught through formulas rather than the process of scientific experimentation, debate, and discovery or by linking these subjects to their broad social implications and historical roots.

If someone claimed that the problem with Auschwitz was that too few inmates had taken character education classes, we would regard this person as mad for failing to understand that the ethical question of the camps concerns the actions of their creators (those with the power to create the context for action) not the behavior of their victims. And yet innumerable people such as former Secretary of Education William Bennett, author of *The Book of Virtues* and confessed high-stakes Las Vegas gambler, want to keep insisting that the economically devastated schools and communities, the crumbling walls, the missing books, the broken heat in urban and rural America — what we really need is classes in character for the students rather than character education classes for the secretaries of education, the policy experts, and the CEOs who earn on average 541 times the average American worker.[45] (In all fairness to the high-rolling William Bennett, he does recognize that schools need more than character education classes. That is why he started a for-profit company called K12 that aims to chisel away at public schools by selling conservative online homeschooling curricula and online virtual charter schools based on the conservative curriculum that he designed.)

The most dilapidated and underfunded U.S. public schools are not concentration camps. Their victims do not face slave labor, starvation, beatings, and near certain death. But the lie of opportunity in wrought iron on the gate of Auschwitz *"Arbeit Macht Frei"* (work shall set you free) is endlessly repeated to students coming from school districts in which nearly all students are living in dire poverty — students who know from experience the truth about lofty promises of opportunities and know from experience the result of how science works to put factories in their neighborhoods, asthma in their chests, and chemicals in their playgrounds, of how English works to keep them out of job interviews and schools, of how history works to lead them off to wars, to segregate cities, to put them into prison, and students know how math works when the wages paid by McDonald's or Wal-Mart do not add up to the cost of a one-bedroom apartment anywhere, and the only opportunities that make sense are the calculated risks of the underground economy.

The George W. Bush Administration's renewed emphasis on standardized testing, coupled with standardization of curriculum, threatens the development of forms of schooling that encourage holistic understandings of how the world works and that foster questioning about how knowledge is created, by whom, and how knowledge relates to broader social questions, problems, power struggles, and individual and social ideals. Reducing teaching and learning to administrative procedures and standardized, quantifiable measures of performance risks eradicating the possibility of students and teachers developing intellectually, and it precludes the possibility that learning makes intellectual engagement the basis for self and social transformation. Should not the value of education be judged by its capacity to make individuals more critical and curious, societies more self-reflective, and the world more ethical? Although too few public schools foster the kinds of democratic education that need to be developed, it is certain that privatizing public schools in general and the Edison model in particular precludes the possibility that such democratic schooling can be developed.

3

EDRON: TWO BRIEF STUDIES IN CORPORATE UNACCOUNTABILITY

"The marketplace theories don't work when you're dealing with this kind of human equation. You don't teach children based on profit margins."

— Kathleen A. Kelley,
President of the Massachusetts Federation of Teachers

One of the most common arguments made by advocates of public school privatization is that the private sector is more "accountable" than the public sector. Edison's operations in Boston and San Francisco paint a different picture.

In the first section of this chapter, I recount the stories of Edison's flagship school Boston Renaissance and the Edison Charter Academy in San Francisco. I then discuss at length how the high expectations and disappointing results at Renaissance were symptomatic of the continuing tendency to understand school accountability through the metaphors of market discipline and physical discipline. Interspersed with the accounts are a number of related discussions about the meaning of test scores, assumptions about race guiding much school reform, and the broad attack on teachers' and women's work. The second section discusses some broader implications of these histories for the corporate and disciplinary models of school accountability including the difference between public and private versions of accountability.

SECTION I: BOSTON AND SAN FRANCISCO

Boston: High Hopes

In 1995, the Boston Renaissance charter school opened in a former office building in downtown Boston, Massachusetts. Renaissance was one of seven for-profit charter schools out of 42 charters opened in the state following an educational reform law in 1993 that allowed for the development of charter schools in the state. Boston Renaissance is the largest charter school in Massachusetts with 1,300 students K–8. "More than half of the students come from disadvantaged families and receive free or reduced-price meals for lunch."[1] It was one of the first four Edison schools and was described as the Edison flagship school. In 2000, school administrators renewed its contract with Edison for five additional years. As of 2001, the school received $12 million for operations. Edison received $9 million of that. Boston Renaissance amounted to the biggest contract Edison had with any school.

Upon its opening, a number of newspapers predicted that Edison's Boston Renaissance would be an educational triumph exemplifying the benefits of the 1993 educational reform law that allowed for the development of charter schools. The *Boston Globe* reported in 1994:

Like other public schools, the charter schools will receive state funding based on how many students they have, but are expected to be centers of innovation because they will be free of school committee and teacher-union oversight and influence. Most of the schools are being opened by teachers, parents, and community groups. "This is the new face of public education," said Chelsea teacher Sarah Kass, cofounder of City on a Hill Charter School in Boston, which will open with 60 high school students. "It tells parents they have a choice."[2]

Although the *Boston Globe* coverage was enthusiastic about the new reform it did mention that there was another perspective on the new reforms.

Critics of charter schools, including some teacher unions and public-school educators, said the charter schools will siphon state dollars meant for public schools. And since each charter school is responsible for student recruitment, critics said it will be easy for them to turn away students perceived as troubled or expensive to educate.[3]

Despite such criticisms by educational researchers, teachers' unions, and others, the general optimism of the *Boston Globe* coverage was shared by *The Washington Post* a year after Renaissance opened. This optimism in the press coverage about Edison came despite a number of prior studies by independent educational researchers suggesting that educational privatization showed little promise of improving quality or decreasing costs. For example, that was the conclusion of a 1992 study of Educational Alternatives Incorporated, by the University of Maryland. The University of Maryland study found that test scores decreased in the first two years of the contract.[4] This conclusion was confirmed by a 1996 study by New York University.[5]

The Washington Post described Renaissance as "brimming with signs of promise."

> Walk the halls and see why: In Bill Gilson's math class, fourth-graders are getting their first dose of fractions and vying to rack up extra points for creating what their teacher calls a "beautiful moment" — when he sees the entire class doing something well. "Like when all of us are raising our hands," says 10-year-old Stephen Myers, "or when we all shut up in the halls."

> Outside Kathy Johnson's classroom, fifth-graders are spending part of their lunch period practicing how to walk single file with arms folded across their chests — a code of conduct the school demands from students whenever they move around the building.[6]

The articles in the *Globe* and the *Post* share more than an optimism about the promise of Renaissance. They share a faith in a discipline-based kind of school reform. If the *Globe* article exemplifies the hope of shifting control away from teachers, teachers' unions, and school committees and toward a for-profit company, the *Post* article exemplifies hope of intensified student discipline as the solution for troubled urban schools.

> The school stresses discipline. And although uniforms are optional, most students wear them. Chatting or running in halls is not tolerated. Teachers serve on "climate committees." Classrooms boast bright posters with examples of model citizenry, such as showing classmates courtesy. Before lunch in Brian Newsom's fourth-grade math class the other day, one student after another raised two fingers above their head — the signal he uses to call for silence. After the entire class settled down, he let them eat.[7]

The strict discipline at Boston Renaissance appears to have been extended to the teachers. "Teachers were trained all at once last year before the school opened and must follow a meticulously outlined curriculum."[8]

Such discipline-oriented reforms in urban public schools presume that the causes of the problems are principally a lack of discipline rather than disparities in funding, lack of adequate resources, broader community problems such as joblessness, poverty, or transience caused by the need for parents to move to obtain work. The charter school movement participates in the broader tendency to identify school problems with a lack of discipline. Charter schools, and particularly for-profit charter schools such as Renaissance, appeared to bring with them the promise of necessary discipline — a discipline thought to be threatened by teacher control over curriculum and teachers' unions.

In 1997, in an editorial, the *Boston Globe* predicted success for Boston Renaissance describing Edison in terms nearly identical with those used on Edison's Web site as a "world-class education from kindergarten through Grade 12" claiming:

> [E]arly results on standardized tests and observation in the classroom suggest strongly that the Renaissance School, like the respected City on a Hill charter school, will be among the triumphs of the Education Reform Act of 1993.[9]

And the editor wrote of Renaissance benefiting from "the luxury of operating free of the administrative and union work rules that often diminish educational opportunity."[10] This prediction of future success for Renaissance came amid a fiscal crisis for the school as it attempted to build space for seventh- and eighth-grade students. The newspaper called on the state legislature to make special concessions for the for-profit school to allow it to receive the same treatment as public schools with regard to eligibility for 50- to 95-percent reimbursement from the state for building improvements. Although the *Globe* suggested that this would only be "fair," the paper did not explain why a company that is taking profits from running a public school should not have to invest income in upkeep or expansion.

Optimism in the press coverage about the future of Renaissance was matched by optimism in the statements from school officials. Headmaster Ester Gliwinski said, "We're able to take all the research that's been done into school reform and do it all at the same time."[11] Gliwinski's hopes for school reform were tied to the capacity to bypass teachers' unions that the charter laws allow: "Part of accountability is, if you are not doing the right job for these children you go away. In public schools you have to live with bad teachers forever."[12] Teachers' unions contend that Edison schools have unacceptable levels of teacher turnover as well as inexperienced teachers. In 1998, Edison teachers had on average only five years of experience versus a national average of sixteen years with a turnover rate of 23 percent.[13]

Ironically, 1998 was the same year that Gliwinski herself "went away," a casualty of high Edison turnover.[14] She was replaced by Roger Harris as headmaster.

Like Gliwinski, Harris was, according to Boston Teachers Union representative Gary Fischer, "not particularly fond of unions."[15] At Harris's prior school, Timilty Middle School in Roxbury, Harris broke union rules by forcing the teachers to work past their schedules without paying them more.[16] Edison's discipline-oriented vision, as well as corporate vision, for the school is apparent in the following profile of Harris:

> He said students booed him at an assembly when he suggested a dress code, but he enlisted their help by setting up essay and art contests. He assured them he did not want them to wear

the plaid jumpers or somber colors often seen in parochial schools.

"I told them I wanted something fresh and funky," he said. What came out of that process was an outfit of chinos, white shirts, and ties. Youngsters who came to school with baggy pants low on their hips with underwear showing were sent to Harris, who used a rope to belt their pants. He laughs now when he describes how he won over those who clung to those baggy pants: He shows coupons supplied by one of the school's business partners, McDonald's, for a free sandwich, drink, and fries. "That won them over," he said.[17]

Harris told students that Michael Jackson wears a uniform, as do the Boston Celtics, the police, and firemen, as part of work.[18] *Globe* correspondent Muriel Cohen mentions that Harris too wore a uniform as a marine in Vietnam. Harris told students, "Even if you go to jail, you'll have to wear a uniform. I told them school was their job and they must dress for success."[19]

Harris' statements to students raise a number of important questions about school reform. Would the disciplinary solutions that Harris put in place in Renaissance be accepted in a suburban school district of largely white professional-class students — the kind of school that would not hire Edison? What kinds of future expectations does Harris' way of thinking assume for students? In a largely white professional-class school would Harris dress students in what reads like Blockbuster video store uniforms — uniforms reminiscent of low-paying non-unionized retail workers? In wealthy communities with strong public schools would Harris suggest prison as a possible future for students, or counterpose prison to working-class jobs or the slim chance of making it in sports or entertainment? For a better understanding of Harris' statements as well as Edison's model and appeal to some people, it is necessary to consider Edison in relation to broader trends in the public conversation about school policy and reform.

Edison can be understood as the culmination of two decades of thinking about school reform through the business and military metaphors of accountability. The dominant strains of accountability thinking go something like this: the real problem facing public schools is not the unequal distribution of educational resources and the fact that poor public schools are in poor neighborhoods that lack jobs, public supports, and private infrastructure. Rather, the real problem with public schools is a lack of discipline. Public administrators are lazy bureaucrats, so goes the logic, who lack the hard discipline of the market to impose the threats of the bottom line. Administrators need to be kept in line by being forced to show measurable, numerically based progress. Treat administrators like CEOs. If they do not deliver, fire them. From this perspective on accountability, teachers lack the discipline and hard work to enforce the proper content knowledge on students. Teachers, so the thinking goes, are protected from being accountable by their unions, which give them job security and help them fight against such reforms as too much testing and scripted lessons, not to mention pay cuts, extended work days, and lengthened work years. The idea is that these protections permit teachers to "get away with not teaching." Students are allowed to "get away without learning" and need to be forced to learn. The solution, according to this logic, is to ramp up discipline on students by testing them more, increase discipline on teachers by giving them scripted lessons and reducing intellectual freedom to plan lessons, and the solution involves threatening administrators with sanctions for not improving test scores. And when test scores do not increase, then punish teachers and students with "reconstitution." In Chicago and other cities, this has meant shuffling teachers around from schools with low scores to other schools with low scores.

The emphasis on accountability defined through discipline brings together military ideals of order with the pro-business ideology of "natural" market efficiency. The pro-business ideology suggests that the failures of public schools have to do with "naturally" inefficient bureaucratic structures characteristic of the public sector more generally. Within this view, the private sector brings profit-seeking behavior that creates competition among students, teachers, and administrators who, when desperately fighting for scarce resources, will learn more material faster.

There are a number of problems with this disciplinary way of thinking about accountability. Some of the more glaring problems are as follows. (1) It wrongly presumes that threats best motivate students to learn, teachers to teach, and administrators to make the best decisions. Most teachers recognize that most students have a natural intellectual curiosity that is sparked by the opportunity to pursue questions and problems that are meaningful to students. (2) The discipline-based ideal of accountability results in a static conception of knowledge as something that others produce and enforce because they know best. It fails to understand knowledge as "in play" and "under construction" and subject to constant revision and reevaluation by teachers and learners. (3) If a democratic society requires dialogue, deliberation, and exchange among citizens, then central educational questions include "Whose voice is heard? Whose knowledge and version of the world counts and whose gets excluded? Who has the power to frame issues and problems, and make claims to truth?" In a highly technological and media-saturated society in which more information is moving faster than ever before and in an economy that is increasingly controlled by fewer massive multinational corporations, it becomes ever more essential to ask questions about who is producing knowledge about such pressing matters as the environment, science, history, politics, war and peace, human values, and education.

There is a conservative political agenda undergirding the discipline-based version of accountability embraced by Edison. For example, No Child Left Behind's emphasis on test-based accountability sets the stage for privatization initiatives. When test scores do not improve, federal and local money will be put toward hiring private consultants when putting the money into the underresourced schools themselves should have been done in the first place. In addition to justifying profit-oriented approaches to public schooling, the approach works to de-link knowledge from questions of its making. The aforementioned social questions that matter to all citizens are not viewed as central to the knowledge students learn in school. Instead, students are taught to think that valuable knowledge magically comes prepackaged in tests and textbooks, somehow determined elsewhere by experts.

Despite the optimistic expectations of physical discipline and "market discipline" that Edison was to bring to Renaissance, despite the optimistic press coverage and the triumphant press releases by Edison, not all was well at Renaissance in conventional terms of academic performance. Although it renewed its contract with Edison for five years in 2000, in 2001 Renaissance scored below average on the statewide Massachusetts assessment tests. By 2002, of eighth grade students, "69% failed the statewide math test, compared with 54% in the Boston school district and 31% in the state; in English, 22% of Renaissance eighth-graders failed, compared with 20% citywide and 8% statewide."[20] The issue of disappointing test performance was not the only one facing Renaissance.

The *American Prospect* reported as early as 1998 that school administrators at Renaissance were being accused of excluding special needs and special education students from the school as a means to raise test scores. Peggy Farber wrote:

> Boston Renaissance's vaunted success may initially have been built in part on an unsavory strategy: in early 1997, Amy Babin,

former coordinator of special education, and other teachers at Boston Renaissance concluded that the school was discouraging families with learning-disabled children from enrolling and was pushing already-enrolled disabled children out of the school. In the days before the first school opened, the principal told Babin that "if we had students who needed resource room-type support, we should counsel the parents that this was not a good match." While it is against federal law to discourage a child's enrollment because of a disability or to avoid providing needed services to an enrolled disabled child, Babin says, "We met with a lot of parents [of disabled children]. The point of the meeting was to discourage them from sending their children."[21]

Admission to Renaissance is by lottery so the alleged exclusion would have had to occur after admission. Farber's article in the *American Prospect* reveals that Renaissance had significantly lower than average enrollments of special education students. The average for Boston schools was 20 percent but Renaissance only had 12 percent special education students, and of students classified as having severe disabilities, Boston averages 10 percent. Renaissance had only one percent of these students. Accusations of Edison counseling out special education and disabled students are not isolated to Renaissance. According to Caroline Grannan of PASA (Parents Advocating School Accountability), this was a widespread practice at Edison schools as a means to raise test scores and decrease costs associated with special provisions.

Charges of counseling out special needs students were flatly denied by Edison. Edison Vice President John Chubb stated, "It is simply not true. It's bad business for us to do anything that suggests we are shortchanging kids."[22] Although Chubb is correct that it would make bad press for this practice to be exposed, there has also been continual intense pressure for Edison to show improved test scores at its schools, especially to maintain continued financial backing from investors. In fact, the company's emphasis on test performance may have been its downfall at Renaissance.

In May 2002, Boston Renaissance severed its relationship with Edison. Although both company and school officials denied that the test scores were the central reason, the *Boston Globe*, no longer so emphatically celebrating the successes of the market model, announced that "the emphasis on standardized testing is also working against Edison. As states develop their own curriculum frameworks and matching exams, the need for outside curricula, like Edison's, is likely to diminish."[23]

Despite a number of press accounts suggesting that test scores were the downfall of Edison, both Edison and the school administration denied that the decline in test scores were responsible for Renaissance ending the contract. The proper place of accountability was a central issue leading to the breaking of the contract. The company and the administration disagreed on where accountability should lie. John Chubb attributed the disappointing test scores to the school board's failure to give the company unlimited control over hiring teachers and in making other instructional decisions. Instead, said Chubb, teachers and administrators were accountable to both the board and Edison. Chubb said:

> [T]he headmaster reported to us, and the headmaster reported to the board. In every other place, the principal reports to us. It was an unusual governance arrangement where the headmaster had two bosses. Frankly, that was confusing.[24]

Chubb also stated:

> That kind of relationship is confusing and suboptimal. Our view was that, if we were going to get the kinds of results in Boston we get everywhere else, we needed more authority.[25]

Chubb's statements are very revealing of how Edison and for-profit schools more generally understand accountability as total control over the school by the corporation. In Boston, Edison was blaming low test scores on public oversight over the company. That is, the company was blaming public accountability, rather than accepting the blame for the low test scores.

Edison's version was very much at odds with the perspective of the school. As Dudley Blodgett, the school's president, put it, "that single point [place] of accountability is an important issue." Blodgett explains that the board was eager to try things "that are outside the Edison model,"[26] including hiring elementary-level teachers specializing in science and hiring two specialists to help new teachers. These priorities of quality were at odds with Edison's designs for the school. If, as Chubb argues, there should be a single place of accountability, then should it not be with the public that the schools serve rather than with the corporation that ultimately seeks to extract profit? For-profit public schools undermine public oversight. Private companies such as Edison can keep their records, much of their accounting, and finances secret, unlike public institutions that are subject to public oversight.

As Boston was deciding to drop Edison, the waiting list for parents to have their kids admitted to the 1,300-student Renaissance school was at 2,200. This fact illuminates two issues. First, as Edison was working toward achieving below average test scores in Boston and around the country, Edison had been for years receiving virtually nothing but praise in the media. This had, in part, to do with the fact that a number of conservative think tanks and policy institutes backed by extremely wealthy patrons had invested heavily in publicity touting the virtues of privatizing public schools. These public relations campaigns helped Edison tremendously as journalists advertised the company as a savior of failed public education. Second, the inadequate investment in improving Boston's public schools fueled the claims of conservative think tanks and public relations companies that the public schools had failed the nation's children. The corporate sector with its "fiscal discipline," particularly in the market-triumphalist 1990s, was being framed in the press as a knight in shining armor for beleaguered public schools beset by the inefficiencies of the public bureaucracy.

Not only in Boston but across the nation, Edison was receiving a barrage of praise in the press as it continued to operate on the corporate model, thus seeming to elevate profit-making and the market as community saviors even as they continued to devastate schools. As Boston was severing its contract with Edison, in Clark County, Nevada the school district began withholding payments to Edison until it fulfilled its promise to obtain large donations from philanthropies. When Edison failed to come through, Clark County dumped Edison too.

> Under its contract with the Clark County district, Edison agreed to raise $1.5 million over three years for each of the seven schools it runs. A $1 million donation was due on Wednesday, but lawyers for Edison and the district say they are still negotiating with the donor.[27]

Should school administrators be forced to worry not only about educating students, issues of curriculm, administration, and finance, but also about the looming possibility that the wheeling and dealing of entrepreneurs will result in fiscal shortage, emergency, and crisis? This kind of uncertainty and instability may be fine for Vegas highrollers, Chicago Board of Trade commodity traders, and Wall Street investment bankers, but it really is not the model for children in public schools.

San Francisco

As Boston Renaissance was breaking its contract, across the nation San Francisco was experiencing accountability the Edison way.

On June 24, 1998 at 12:30 in the morning in a middle school auditorium filled with placard-carrying parents and teachers, the San Francisco school board voted to allow the Edison Project to run a public elementary school, coincidentally named Edison Elementary. The contentious five-to-two vote was under scrutiny the next day by district lawyers because one of the board members, Keith Jackson, had technically resigned from the board effective at midnight — a half hour before the vote. The two members opposed to Edison taking over the school under a charter agreement were Jill Wynns and Dan Kelly, who insisted that more public debate was necessary before letting "a company with a questionable record" take over the school.[28] Although Wynns attempted to filibuster the vote until after midnight by introducing 13 amendments to the decision, Superintendent Bill Rojas and the board members in favor of the contract insisted that the vote should count despite the inclusion of Jackson's dubious vote. The charter agreement that was decided by the vote, as at Boston Renaissance, would mean that the school would be public, but would not be subject to some state and local rules — most notably, Edison would not allow new teachers to join the teachers' union.

In the summer of 1999, *The San Francisco Chronicle* published an effusive article by an elementary school principal named Ken Romines about how the new Edison Charter Academy was a spectacular success owing to the freedom that charter schools have to partner with business. Romines, who had served as the principal of Edison Elementary from 1993–1995, described students as little entrepreneurs about their learning (students were learning to be "independent learners," the reading materials were "student-managed") and attributed the change in the school's approach to reading to the partnership among parents, educational, community, and business leaders. Romines repeated that the students were learning the "value" and "joy" of literacy and learning. The accompanying photograph showed a kindergarten teacher telling students to think before answering a money-counting exercise.[29] Romines concluded:

> Edison Charter Academy is an important example of how a collaboration of committed parents with educational, community, and business leaders can lead school change. I think these students will succeed. That is, if we continue to give their families and their new school the time and opportunity they deserve.[30]

Why was Romines arguing in 1999, so early in its contract, for Edison to be allowed to continue? Because by December 1998, only half way through its first year, the teachers' union, United Educators of San Francisco, filed a grievance against the district for requiring its teachers at Edison Charter Academy to work consistently longer hours for the same pay. According to the union's calculations, Edison was demanding that its teachers work a seven percent longer work year without a corresponding pay increase. As a result of these longer hours, by the end of Edison's first year managing the school, 21 of 26 teachers left. In the summer of 2000, the school board threatened to revoke the charter twice over labor disputes.

Edison barely avoided a massive teacher walkout at Edison Charter Academy at the beginning of the 2000–2001 school year. Two-thirds of the school's 33 teachers planned to quit. Although the Edison teachers nationwide were typically earning about five to 10 percent more than public school teachers according to the company, teachers at Edison Charter Academy were working 10- to 12-hour days for just a few thousand dollars more.[31] Teacher Kathy Fleming estimated she had worked 42 days for free. With this in mind she decided, along with 26 other teachers at the school, to write a letter asking their elected officials to intervene. Facing threats by the school board of having their contract revoked, Edison offered the overworked teachers a 10 percent pay increase over union rates and in so doing avoided losing its contract with the district. Unfortunately, this was not enough for the teachers: all but seven left ECA after the second year, not including the principal.

The threat of an interrupted school year was not a result of malicious or undisciplined teachers but rather was the result of an underregulated situation in which the company was not held accountable for its labor practices. To be treated fairly as public school teachers, Edison's teachers had to hold the company accountable by threatening to walk out.

Accountability as the Undermining of Teacher Work

One way that privatizers justify their actions is by claiming that privatizing public schools increases parental involvement and encourages kids to take responsibility for their own learning. A prominent op-ed piece appeared in *The San Francisco Chronicle* on June 10, 1999, by a parent singing the praises of Edison for accomplishing just these goals. Myrna Banks, a volunteer and parent at Edison Charter Academy wrote, "Kids are taking responsibility for their own learning…. One of the biggest changes is that parental involvement is encouraged."

These ideas would suggest that privatization increases local control over the schooling process despite that control actually shifts to corporate headquarters — in the case of Edison, New York City. Privatization advocates may be concerned less with "parental involvement and children taking responsibility for themselves" than with using unpaid parent and student labor to replace paid and unionized labor for such necessities as janitorial services and administration. Chris Whittle saw the market potential of putting kids to work in schools early in the planning for the Edison Project. He discussed the role of children, not just parents, in taking on various jobs in the schools. These included janitorial work. As Edison was facing multiple problems in the spring of 2002, Whittle returned to such pronouncements that costs could be cut by having school children do expensive administrative work. Bizarrely, Whittle gave numerical conversions for how many school kids equal a single school administrator! It turns out that by Whittle's logic, 600 school kids working one hour a day equals 75 full-time adult staff.

Caroline Grannan of San Francisco–based PASA pointed out that Whittle was really calling for a return to child labor. Grannan was not the only one to make such an observation. One sixth-grader in Philadelphia, Janet McCoy, at Edison-run Gillespie Middle School stated, "It's wrong for them to use students as free labor when we come to school to learn." The news release by one organization fighting Edison in Philadelphia highlighted the racist implications of Whittle's solution: "over 90% of the students in Edison's Philadelphia Schools are children of color.... 'Is Chris Whittle suggesting that our children make up his modern day school plantation?' said Helen Gym of Asian Americans United."[32] Indeed, one wonders how would parents and students in the wealthiest and whitest public school districts in the nation respond to similar proposals.

When such proclamations are made about the virtues of "parental involvement," what is typically assumed is that this is going to be the free labor of mothers and female guardians. Whom exactly do Whittle and other advocates of volunteerism have in mind? The school parking lot lined with the convertible Jaguars and Lexuses and Mercedes SUVs of the fine ladies of Newton, Massachusetts, Farmington, Connecticut, Bethesda, Maryland, New Trier, Illinois, and Marin County, California traipsing into schools to hang their fur coats on the hooks by the cubbies to scrub floors and clean toilets? Caroline Grannan put it quite succinctly in summarizing the assumption about class made by the privatizers. She asks, "How many empowered middle-class parents would consider sending their kids to an Edison school?"[33]

The talk of kids taking responsibility for their own learning and of parents being involved in local schools through volunteering is part of the larger call on the part of conservatives for the transformation of universally provided public services to voluntary organizations. Like Colin Powell's call for volunteerism, the George W. Bush Administration's "faith-based" initiatives are part of this attempt to shift responsibility for social service provision away from guarantees on universal provisions for such public services as education, health care, welfare and toward local and voluntary provisions for such services. This shifting of control and administration for delivery of these services away from the federal government through block grants to states was begun during Clinton under the auspices of Republican leadership in Congress, essentially making social responsibility a private matter. The emphasis on local control has been part of a long, ugly tradition of promoting self-determination through the Confederate legacy of states' rights. At the same time conservatives use the rhetoric of volunteerism to suggest that federal- and state-funded social services should be defunded and replaced by faith-based, business-based, and volunteer-based initiatives. Conservatives shift the onus of responsibility for public service provision from society onto individuals (mostly women) while they simultaneously work hard to make private investment risk by the wealthy everyone's fiscal responsibility. The way the public is being forced to insure the profits of the airline and insurance industries following September 11 exemplifies this trend. By the logic of volunteerism, individual Americans are responsible for the state of their own communities but all Americans are responsible for helping massive corporations keep profits flowing to their CEOs. Considering the radical increases in CEO pay relative to the steady decline in real wages over the past three decades, this particular form of socialism for the rich is exceptionally obscene.

In the 2000–2001 school year there were two plans afoot at the San Francisco school board to revoke the charter in light of the labor dispute. One plan, co-sponsored by board president and Edison supporter Mary Hernandez, called for returning the school to district control if the labor dispute was not resolved by September 12. Jill Wynns authored a different plan that called for immediate termination of the contract. The walkout was averted when Edison agreed to "an 11th hour, 10 percent salary boost to keep teachers from quitting en masse."[34] Although the contract was not revoked in 2000 this would not be the last upheaval at Edison Charter Academy that year.

Despite the labor strife, things were looking up for Edison in San Francisco when in the fall of 2000, Edison Charter Academy became one of eight out of a hundred schools in the city that qualified for state cash tied to test score performance on the Academic Performance Index. Edison Charter Academy tested 95 percent of its students. Embracing a business model of cash incentives, the state promised schools $150 per student, employee bonuses, and additional bonuses of $25,000, $10,000, or $5,000 per teacher at schools designated as low performing that make the largest gains in test scores. Despite that 67 percent of California schools were to receive money in January 2000, only 11 percent of the San Francisco schools were to receive money. Nanette Asimov, of the San Francisco Chronicle wrote:

> For many years, Edison was among the city's worst-performing schools. Two years ago, the coincidentally named Edison Corp. took over the school, which remained public, installed a new curriculum and began working its teachers longer hours. Public school purists cried foul. They said the company would drive out low-income children. And they were gleeful last spring when Edison teachers rebelled against longer schedules that did not include more pay.... Although its test scores remain low, they

are better than last year's. At the school 70 percent of students are low-income, and 29 percent are learning to speak English.[35]

Although Asimov hailed Edison for its accomplishment, she did not question the underlying assumptions about this way of distributing much-needed resources to the city's public schools. By linking cash rewards to test score improvement, the state was suggesting that the reason for low test score performance had to do with a lack of incentives. The carrot would be more resources for the school, and the stick would be the withholding of the needed extra resources. Disparities in test performance as well as the quality of education throughout the local, state, and nation align neatly with the class position of the students' families.[36] Hence, when much needed extra cash is denied to schools enrolling poorer students, a self-fulfilling prophecy is realized. Essentially, such a system rewards privileged students while making everyone teach to the test. Tests such as the Academic Performance Index measure not only what is learned in school but also what students bring from their social milieu outside of school. Conversely, the tests do not measure and hence do not value the knowledge brought to school by nondominant-culture and nondominant-language students. For example, the tests do not reward degrees of bilingual achievement or the cultural knowledge attained by students of minority cultures. Nor do the tests help teachers, students, administrators, or parents engage in dialogue and debate about what knowledge is valuable for students to learn and how different knowledge relates to the different interests and perspectives of different students. Such dialogue and debate enable communities to deliberate about public priorities and hence serve as an indispensable part of democratic practice.

In *The San Francisco Chronicle*, debate raged over the meaning of the test scores. The paper published a series of editorials by school board member and Edison opponent Mark Sanchez, who argued that the test scores at Edison improved because the population of the school changed. He also stated that Edison was operating "on the backs of new teachers," referring to the high teacher turnover and the heavy reliance on new teachers to staff the schools cheaply.[37] Debra J. Saunders assailed Sanchez and his fellow board member Jill Wynns in the paper, claiming that the "numbers demonstrate "significant" improvement in reading and math."[38]

As Dana Woldow pointed out in response to Saunders, "similar or more substantial gains occurred at numerous other San Francisco schools serving disadvantaged students, including Bret Harte, Flynn, Bryant and Malcolm X."[39]

PASA issued a press release in the summer of 2001 stating that, despite that Edison was claiming to include 95 percent of its students in its tests, it was excluding about 25 percent of African American students from its test scores.[40] The press release claims a disparity between the inclusion of African American students at Edison Charter Academy and other San Francisco schools tested.

Accusations of racism such as those leveled by PASA mostly involved charges of the company "counseling out" black students. However, the claims about discipline-based accountability that Edison uses to sell its services are wrapped up in a much deeper, more profound form of racism. The metaphor of discipline is commonly used to justify repressive conditions in poorer, less-white schools — these include surveillance cameras, ID card dog tags, police presence, sniffing-dogs, transparent backpacks, and strict rules governing bodily movement and speech. Despite that the vast majority of high-profile school shootings such as Columbine occur in predominantly white schools, black schools are targeted for the most repressive measures. The racially charged language of discipline and accountability participates in a broader cultural racism that wrongly blames nonwhite citizens for the historical underfunding of

nonwhite schools and communities while exonerating privileged citizens who have benefited from unequal resource allocation.

It is important to recognize both that the schools targeted for
privatization are predominantly nonwhite and that the schools
most targeted for discipline are nonwhite. In Chester, Pennsylvania a Republican-controlled state seized a predominantly nonwhite poor school and installed a white retired Marine Corps
Colonel named Tom Persing. Colonel Persing promptly turned
the school over to Edison. In Baltimore, Edison hired retired
administrator Sarah Horsey to run Montibello elementary. She
is shown in a PBS *Frontline* documentary about Edison called
"Public Education, Inc.," marching very young black students
in the schoolyard. The students are outfitted in full military
fatigues while other students are shown responding to her in
the call-and-response style of military boot camp. Disciplinarian
Sarah Horsey is black and Colonel Tom Persing is white. The fact
that they both represent the embrace of strict discipline for
school and student success does not suggest that school discipline is "racially neutral." School discipline is a racialized ideology that is informed by a set of broader assumptions about
economic success, race, and behavior. Generally, the ideology
of school discipline suggests that student success is principally
a matter of successfully following rules of conduct. In the ideology of school discipline, the rules of individual conduct are
symbolically aligned with a number of characteristics historically associated with whiteness: reserve, order, rationality, emo-
tional restraint, control, precision, technological mastery, etc.
These characteristics are not only historically associated with
whiteness but they are also defined against those characteristics
historically attributed to nonwhites at the lower rungs of the
racial hierarchy: laziness, irrationality, animality, emotionalism,
physicality. Most importantly, the ideology of school discipline
functions in the interests of currently existing configurations of

racialized class power by framing out of consideration the ways that student success has much to do with both class position and the distribution of cultural capital — that is, culturally valued knowledge, speech codes, and affect that tend to be differentially aligned with race and class.

The "Public Schools, Inc." documentary and a number of newspaper accounts illustrate how Edison blamed its failure at Dodge Elementary School in Wichita, Kansas as principally caused by predominantly nonwhite students lacking discipline. In the documentary, teachers and administrators at Dodge explain that, on the contrary, the principal problem at Dodge had to do with Edison putting too much of its attention, time, and resources toward getting new business to make the company grow rather than on improving the quality of the school.

Despite the alleged racial manipulations in San Francisco in 2000, Edison's scores were far below district-wide average. These are the scores based on national percentile ranking for average student score[41]:

Grade:	2	3	4	5
Reading:	District 56; Edison 33	D 46; E 28	D 51; E 30	D 47; E 35
Math:	District 65; Edison 57	D 62; E 41	D 57; E 32	D 59; E 49

As the test score dispute continued, another feud erupted over the school board election.

Fishy Elections

Gap clothing company (which includes Old Navy and Banana Republic) owner Don Fisher, who had invested in Edison stock and given grants to Edison schools in San Francisco, was found to be funneling money into the school board election campaign in the direction of pro-Edison board members through a political consulting firm called Barnes, Mosher, Whitehead and Partners (known as BMW).[42] The consulting firm was funding a front group called "San Franciscans for Sensible Government" that was distributing school board election campaign flyers that advertised pro-Edison incumbents: Mary Hernandez, Stephen Herman, and Robert Varni. The outcome of the hard-fought board race would likely determine whether or not the board would break the contract with Edison. Because the flyers were not authorized by any of the candidates, they did not fall under the city's campaign finance rules, which allow a maximum individual donation of $500. This arrangement earned them the informal title of a "soft money" donation. The price tag on this "soft money" donation was $47,100 — substantially more than any individual candidate raised for the entire campaign.[43]

> Asked why she thought the soft money filtered down into school board politics this year, Wynns said, "It's about Edison. I can't see any other thing that it's about." Fisher was not available to comment said a spokeswoman. Mosher of BMW did not return several calls. Hernandez declined to comment.[44]

The flyers were not enough to convince the voters in San Francisco to vote the way of the Edison boosters. The election resulted in the reelection of Wynns as well as a new antiprivatization majority of four to three on the San Francisco Unified School Board. Defenders of the soft money contribution for the election, including incumbents Stephen Herman and Robert Varni, argued that if the unions were allowed to fund candidates such as Wynns, Eric Mar, and Mauricio Vela, then the advocates of privatization should be allowed to fund their candidates also.

> But Mar argued that the teacher money is different. "Unions are made up of thousands of dues-paying members. Leadership is usually democratically elected and held accountable through these elections by its membership," he said via e-mail while participating in an online forum in which scores of parents,

candidates and teachers discuss the city schools. "Corporations are essentially only accountable to a handful of wealthy individuals."⁴⁵

Herein lies a key difference of perspective as to where accountability is best generated. For advocates of public schools, democratic governance should assure accountability. For advocates of privatization, accountability is the result of the movement of the market. Chris Whittle put it quite succinctly with reference to San Francisco:

"If you run good schools, there shouldn't be this issue," Whittle said last week. "If you don't run good schools, you get fired. In San Francisco, we may get fired for running a good school."⁴⁶

In the end, Edison was fired by the new San Francisco Board of Education. However, before ending the contract, the board issued a report with a conclusion very different from Whittle's about the quality of Edison Charter Academy.

The scathing report, the result of a month-long investigation, was issued on March 27, 2001. Allegations in the report include special education students were "counseled to leave Edison"; "some parents were told that Edison "was not the place" for their children"⁴⁷; the company also failed to provide the district with financial records that track spending of public money, particularly expenditures to help low-income students; parents of African American students "were told that Edison might not be "the right school" for them, and said the school's teachers and staff treated black students differently from students of other ethnicities [sic]"⁴⁸; teachers testified they were victims of "extreme coercion" to sign a petition in support of the original charter. The report also found several violations of the charter agreement by the company. These included "high teacher turnover created by difficult working conditions; inadequate bilingual programs; a nonexistent parent and community oversight committee; and the replacement of a free after-school program with an Edison program that costs parents $200 a month.... The report states that Edison received 'almost a million dollars more from the district than it spent at (the school)' in the 1999–2000 school year." [49]

The board voted 6 to 1 that Edison had to either fix these problems in 90 days or lose the contract.

Edison officials responded by denying the charges and accusing the district of bias. They did not, however, satisfy the demands of the board in the time allotted. On June 28, 2001, the board ended the contract. This was the first contract Edison lost. It has since lost 18 more.

The state of California Board of Education bailed out the company, offering Edison a state contract to run the school autonomously a month later.

> Under the new agreement, Edison will begin paying the school district rent, estimated to be around $300,000 a year. Edison also agreed to give up about $300,000 a year it has received from the district in annual desegregation funds. The school district will pay for student busing for two years, and teachers will become Edison corporation employees. Tenured teachers will have two years to return to a district school if they choose. First-year teachers will have one year to decide. [50]

The senior vice president of Edison Gaynor McCown stated that she was relieved that a compromise was reached. [51]

School board members were not so thrilled with the outcome despite succeeding at ending the contract. Board member Dan Kelly described it not as a victory but rather as a truce. [52] Board President Wynns stated, "This has been a long, difficult process, one that has not always been characterized by respectable behavior." "This agreement is the best we can get. It makes

Edison a separate school district within the county of San Francisco."[53]

SECTION II: LESSONS ABOUT ACCOUNTABILITY

Public Oversight Versus Private Profit

The Boston and San Francisco experience with Edison highlights the private version of accountability as opposed to a public version of accountability. Part of what makes public administration and control over public services distinct is public oversight. This means that part of what assures the quality of public services is that the public is watching and keeping track of how public money is being spent, what the agenda is, and how the agenda aligns with public values and goals.

Like Whittle and Chubb, Thomas Toch, who works for the National Center for Education and the Economy, claims that profit motive is the real guarantor of quality. Says Toch:

> I am not an apologist for Edison but this is a very difficult business.... Edison critics say they can do everything Edison can do by themselves without the specter of profit-making. The simple fact is that rarely happens.[54]

Typical of conservative privatization advocates, Toch believes that the profit motive is what keeps the public in check. Every good public school in the nation attests to the glaring falseness of Toch's claim that quality schools rarely result without profit motive. As Stephanie Salter wrote in *The San Francisco Chronicle*:

> To be sure, there is much in this nation's public school systems that needs fixing. (There is much that works, but no one ever talks about that.) Given the vicissitudes of the free market, it seems pretty dumb to me to put the repair job into the hands

> of people whose primary mission is not to enlighten little Billy
> and Sue, but to keep the stockholders smiling. Especially peo-
> ple who have to borrow at 20 percent.[55]

None of the best public schools in the nation is constrained by
the concerns of investors worried about their profits, nor questions whether the school will have to close up shop, nor questions whether overworked parents will need to volunteer to
clean the cafeteria, nor questions whether little kids will have
to work as administrators. What most consider the best public
schools in the nation are heavily funded through lavish property
taxes, and such schools benefit by having parents who are in
positions of political power and influence so that if there are
any shortcomings at the school, the administration and school
board and city officials will hear about it. In other words, the
model of public oversight is clearest in places with the most
power and wealth. This suggests that in places where public
oversight is weaker, it should be strengthened rather than undermined through privatization initiatives.

While Toch makes the dubious argument that privatization
ensures accountability, an argument that the national experience
with Edison seems to refute, he also makes the argument that
direct public involvement in school policy as a form of oversight
undermines the capacity of the for-profit company to deliver
accountability. As the public took to the streets to demonstrate
against Edison taking over the Philly schools, Toch responded
by saying:

> It is making it very difficult for them [Edison] with potential
> investors who get gun-shy in the face of demonstrators in the
> streets of Philadelphia.[56]

Poor Edison and those poor investors whose profits could be
interrupted by teachers, students, and administrators who do

not want their schools turned into an enterprise zone! Of course, this kind of direct action for public oversight tends to happen in places where political power is weakest and public oversight cannot operate through the normal channels of bureaucracy. This way of thinking about oversight by Toch and his ilk really amounts to a disdain for the public, a perspective that the public gets in the way of democratic control over public institutions. In this perspective, democracy is a game for elites and the public interest is indistinguishable from the private pursuit of profit. This is quite at odds with how the protesters feel.

Toch, a former journalist who happens to be regularly interviewed in newspapers as an educational expert, should not be taken very seriously as a public school policy spokesperson simply because, like Chubb, Finn, Giuliani, and other advocates of privatization, he is financially invested in what he is championing as good policy. The National Center for Education and the Economy hawks "standards-based" educational products in conjunction with educational publishers. This conflict of interest raises the question of how corporate media select advocates of corporate schooling to speak as experts on school reform. There is a tremendous danger to democratic deliberation on issues of public import when control over information is dominated by for-profit media. Likewise, the privatization of public schools reduces the range of information that students will be able to access to that information compatible with the views acceptable to the private sector. It is no coincidence that Toch's organization pushes "standards-based" curricula. Such programs have a conservative ideological perspective that disconnects knowledge from broader issues, social contexts, histories, and power struggles and reduces knowledge to units of truth to be passively consumed. This is not to suggest that public schools today offer an adequately wide range of perspectives and sufficiently encourage students to question knowledge in relation to democratic concerns with power, politics, and justice. However, privatizing public school guarantees that subjugation of education to the narrow dictates of a small number of citizens who control the economy; it does not explore the possibilities of education that serves the interests of the bulk of the citizenry.

The very framing of the educational reform debates in the language of the market, with terms such as "accountability," "public monopoly," "competition," and "efficiency," makes a business model appear commonsensical despite that goals and assumptions derived from the private sector do not apply to public schooling. This kind of language has overrun not only much of the academic conversation but also the public conversation found in such mainstream press as The Washington Post. Referring to PASA's Caroline Grannan, the Post writes, "some customers have not been satisfied." What the Post's language highlights is the ways that within the business language citizens can be conceived of only as consumers. This shifts the discussion and commonsense language so that it becomes increasingly difficult to think about school reform in terms of public provision and instead it becomes increasingly natural to think about school as just another consumable commodity like fast food or toilet paper.

We are told every day by a barrage of television, radio, film, and internet information, that our individual freedom is maximized by our capacity as consumers. It only makes sense then to think of parents choosing schools as the most free and hence most democratic way to allocate school resources. Of course, part of what this perspective misses is that the range of available choices is being set before individual parents have the opportunities to choose. In other words, parents in the Mission district of San Francisco are not offered a choice of elite private schools. And, of course, they are also not offered a choice of incomes, a choice of neighborhoods to live in, a choice of levels of public and private infrastructure in their communities, or a choice of how they are viewed, valued, and represented by those in society with the most power. By describing school as a business and relying on the idea of freedom as freedom to shop, conservatives have been very successful in convincing some of the poorest parents that school choice is really an opportunity rather than a poor substitute for proper investment in public schools as part of an investment in the public that is necessary to achieve democratic participation and universal welfare.

This way of thinking about school as a business may not foster the kind of education that helps students develop the tools to participate in a democratic society. But that may not be what some of Edison's biggest supporters from the private sector have in mind. In San Francisco, Don Fisher gave $25 million to Edison. Fisher and his family own the Gap and its many subsidiary retail clothing stores such as Banana Republic and Old Navy. The Fishers have come under fire from activists for using overseas sweatshop factories known to employ child labor. The Fisher family has been invested in logging old-growth forests on the West Coast. Some of the trees that the Fishers want to turn into lumber are not just older than the Gap. They are older than the United States of America. The Gap has also taken heat for its advertising campaigns such as its ads for Khakis. These ads showcase unique historical figures wearing brown pants. The ad copy reads, "Hemingway wore Khakis." The ads sell the ultimate conformist garment by suggesting their exclusivity and distinctness. Ridiculing the campaign, the magazine *Adbusters* ran a spoof with accompanying picture, "Hitler wore khakis." The further point suggested by the *Adbusters* spoof is how consumption carries no ethical content. Likewise, consumption as the model for school reform (Edison consumers) or as the justification for an education (get good grades, get a good job, buy a lot of stuff) lacks the ethical dimension of education that has historically been central to the way schooling has been conceived — namely, education makes an individual who can act ethically and who can contribute to making society better. While consumption as the basis for schooling may have no ethical content, it certainly does carry with it political implications — distinctly conservative ones.

No Politically Neutral Model of Accountability

The right-wing *National Review* blames the failures of Edison in San Francisco on a school board packed with "reactionary left-wing" ideologues. This came in a defense of Edison amid charges that it "got rid of" black students and special education students in hopes of showing higher test scores and cutting costs on special education. The broader point about accountability here is that the right-wing accuses liberals and progressives of having an ideological agenda in defense of bloated bureaucracy and at the expense of school kids. So what the market does, from this conservative perspective, is offer a "non-ideological" basis for school reform. When the *National Review* points to rising test scores in Edison's San Francisco schools (scores that were lower increases relative to the rest of the district increases and scores that later significantly fell), they are appealing to the common sense of efficacy — that is, "whatever works." And for privatization advocates, the market always works even when it does not work, hence the need to blame protesters, students, teachers, administrators, and the public sector generally, as Toch does. When liberals accept these basic ground rules of "whatever works" for thinking about public schools, they inadvertently play into the hands of conservatives.

Gerald Bracey, Peter Cookson, Alex Molnar, Alfie Kohn, Henry Levin, Amy Stuart Wells, David Berliner, Carol Ascher, and a number of other important liberal and progressive scholars have provided tremendous insights into the empirical failings of privatization experiments. They have also shown how right-wing claims are often misleading and more ideologically motivated than grounded in empirical evidence. However, many liberal educational scholars have tended to underemphasize or even deny the extent to which education is thoroughly ideological from the curriculum choices to the funding structure to the ways that different subjects are taught. When liberal scholars ground claims against Edison in terms of the threat posed to "a quality education," they tend not to explore adequately what "a quality education" means, that its meaning is struggled over by different groups with different and competing material interests and cultural values. The wholesale embrace of the empirical evidence as a means of refuting the conservative claims tends to be viewed by liberal scholars as an expedient and pragmatic approach to intervening in the public conversation about privatization. One must be sympathetic to the liberal approach to battling expediently the privatizers with the common sense of numbers — especially considering the amount of money pouring into conservative, pro-privatization think tanks. However, one progressive policy expert, Pauline Lipman, summed up the problem with the liberal approach this way, "what if privatization really did mean higher test scores? Would liberals then embrace it?" What Lipman's question highlights is the panoply of other issues that are erased by the embrace of efficacy and the extent to which efficacy-oriented thought is at odds with fundamentally liberal values.

For example, liberals tend to embrace collaborative learning, equality of educational provision, learning thought of as a process, holism, and multiculturalism to name but a few practices. The rise of the conservative standards and accountability movement, with its test obsession, and the need to quantify and measure all achievement undermine liberal approaches that aim for liberal values. So when liberals, for pragmatic reasons of effectively entering policy debates, base their criticisms on general statements about quality education (assumed to be measurable by test scores), first, they fail to admit their own ideological perspective and, second, they undermine the very basis to challenge the ideological perspective of their right-wing foes.

Popular press and academic writing on privatization reveals that both liberals and conservatives want to deny their ideologies and claim an impossible neutrality and an impossible objectivity. So when Chris Whittle dismisses Edison's problems in San Francisco as "nothing more than ideological interference," he is being consistent with the ridiculous right-wing claims that there is no ideological agenda undergirding his attempts to privatize public schools. Karen Breslau and Nadine Joseph writing in *Newsweek* point out:

> Whittle still tends to dismiss his critics as "leftist" bureaucrats blinded by a hatred of his bottom-line approach. There may be an element of truth to that in liberal bastions like San Francisco or New York, where parents recently blocked Edison's attempt to take over five schools. But it doesn't play well in Sherman, Texas, where the school board decided last year not to renew Edison's contract, citing poor student performance and hidden costs.[57]

The point that Breslau and Joseph make is well taken, but they are nonetheless viewing claims about ideological motivations as distinct from whether or not Edison "works." The very idea that Edison could "work" is itself ideological in that it presumes that many political ideals are settled that are still contentious and heavily debated, like what a quality education is, what public education should do, why kids should be in public schools at all, etc. Public school accountability should involve open public discussion and debate about what values and beliefs are implicit in curriculum and governance so that public schools can be a vibrant and democratic place that also model democratic participation for students.

4

NO CONTEST: EDISON'S TAKEOVER OF THE PHILADELPHIA SCHOOLS AND THE LESSONS OF PUBLIC SCHOOL COMPETITION

Running schools is the heart of the game.

— Chris Whittle

One parent of a five-year-old daughter put it this way referring to Edison's operations in Philadelphia, "I don't consider putting 15,000 students with a company that can't guarantee operations next year reform. It's not just a stock game, this is my child's life."[1]

INTRODUCTION

On the morning of November 29, 2001, hundreds of Philadelphia students walked out of classes and joined other protesters in the street to march on school district headquarters. Students from Mastbaum, William Penn, and other schools held signs aloft while chanting, "Keep Schools Public!"[2] As the students descended on headquarters, they were confronted by a phalanx of plainclothes police officers in trench coats and armbands that read "police." The officers were blocking the entrance to the school board building at 21st Street and Ben Franklin Parkway as the school board planned to meet for what might have been the last time.

After school, hundreds of student activists led by the Philadelphia Student Union marched down the Parkway to hold a formal protest at City Hall.

> They chanted, "Hey, hey! Ho ho! Edison has got to go," and "It's not hard, it's not funny, all the other kids have money. Like the kids across the nation, we just want our education." To symbolize their desire to keep Edison out of the Philadelphia system, they grasped hands and formed a human chain around the entire building.[3]

These were not the first protests by students, parents, teachers, and many citizens who were up in arms over the state of Pennsylvania's seizure of the Philadelphia public schools from the city due to occur on November 30, 2001.

The prior summer, in August 2001, Governor Tom Ridge had ordered an evaluation of the city schools by Edison. Ridge stated, "It is designed not to point fingers, but to suggest fresh ideas and innovative perspectives for the district."[4] A month later the events of September 11 resulted in the governor being courted as the first secretary of the George W. Bush Administration's newly created Department of Homeland Security. Plans laid by Ridge for the state to seize the city's schools went forward and that November newly installed Pennsylvania governor Mark Schweiker (Ridge's lieutenant governor) led the takeover. The plan was to dissolve the city board of education and replace the management of the city schools with the Edison Schools corporation.

> Experts say the plan, approved under a state law, is the most radical reform ever tried in a large public school system. No other urban school system has seen such widespread privatization coupled with almost total state control.[5]

Schweiker's plan called for a for-profit management company, likely Edison, to run the system and directly run 60 city schools in partnerships with universities, businesses, religious institutions, or politicians. The top 55 city administrators were to be fired and replaced by managers hired by the for-profit company. Other parts of the proposal included the following:

> Principals in other schools would collect bonuses as large as 30 percent if they raise student test scores, while as many as 1,500 teachers would be offered $7,500 raises to serve as mentors for less experienced colleagues. The initiatives would be funded with an annual infusion of $150 million to the system's $1.7 billion budget — half from the state and half from the cash-strapped city. The state is recommending a $300 million bond issue to refinance the district's operating debt and calling for a separate investment of $100 million in the worst schools. Students would be given 1 million new textbooks and $51 million would be spent to spruce up the city's 264 schools, more than half of which are at least 60 years old. To help pay for the plan, the school system's headquarters building would be sold.[6]

In 1998, the state legislature had passed a compromise law setting the stage for the state to take over school districts. The law was a compromise with Governor Tom Ridge who had been pushing hard for a voucher system in the state.

As a Republican governor with both houses of the state legislature in Republican control, Governor Ridge came to office counting on a full range of methods to use in school reform, up to and including vouchers. His first voucher proposal failed, as did his second and third. Members of the Ridge camp were stoic at first. But as the years rolled on, they began to criticize fellow Republicans who refused to extend their free-market philosophies to the education field. As one state official said earlier this month, "The unpleasant secret is that some in our party oppose vouchers because they don't want poor children from the inner city coming into their neighborhoods to go to school."[7]

The legislation gave sweeping power to the state to take over and refashion districts where more than half of students failed reading and math exams administered by the state. Initially, the law was used against Chester Upland school district. The state-appointed board hired three for-profit companies: Edison, Mosaica, and LearnNow. Retired Marine Corps Colonel Thomas Persing, the chair of the board overseeing Upland, warned, "There is no light switch out there you can turn on and off" to save foundering school systems.[8] Although on the eve of the state seizure of Philadelphia, Persing did not comment on the academic performance of Edison, he did grade the company a "C+" by other measures:

"At some schools, supplies have been late to arrive," he said. "Edison also has lagged behind in completing government paperwork and," he added, "has shown limited understanding of rules governing federal funds."[9]

By mid-November 2001, it was not only students who were protesting the move by the state to hand management of the city schools over to Edison. Mayor John Street set up an emergency office in the school board building in mid-November. Street publicly complained that Edison had an inside track for the big contract in Philadelphia because Edison had been commissioned by Ridge for the study and was paid nearly $3 million for it. Street commented, "Bringing in a company with no reasonable experience to run a system of this magnitude is just short of foolhardy."[10] Meanwhile the American Federation of Teachers, the parent organization of the Philadelphia teachers' union published a study of Edison's performance that disputed Edison's claims of superior academic achievement, finding instead that Edison's performance is comparable with or worse than that of other public schools.

Events took a surprising turn when on November 20, 2001, Governor Schweiker announced that the state would not seek to install Edison to replace the top 55 administrators in Philadelphia. Despite the pullback from installing Edison to run the city schools, the state went ahead with the rest of the plans, including shutting down the city school board building, moving forward on a major role for Edison, and appointing a panel that would name a "chief executive with a strong business background to manage the 260-school system."[11] It was these plans that protesters were opposing on the march of November 29. Prior protests by students, parents, and unions as well as the mayor's intervention had clearly been instrumental in Schweiker's reversal.

> As the Dec. 1 deadline that the governor had set for the takeover approached, the city had appeared on the brink of revolt. Hundreds of parents and community leaders began gathering to organize mass protests at the state Capitol in Harrisburg as well as student walkouts. At times, some opponents cast the fight in racial terms, saying that a largely Black and Hispanic school system was under siege from a heavily white state government.... The surprise decision, announced after hours of

secret talks with the mayor at a law firm in Philadelphia, was a setback for Edison. It is the second time this year that parents have helped cut back the company plans. Earlier, parents in five New York City public schools voted resoundingly to bar Edison from taking control of their classrooms.[12]

Despite Schweiker's retreat on Edison running the city schools in November, on December 22, 2001 Schweiker and Street revealed an agreement involving Edison as a system-wide consultant and possible manager of 60 of 260 schools. As part of the deal, the mayor-appointed board of education was suspended indefinitely while the governor committed to $75 million of a $2 billion annual budget that leaked $200 million annually in operational deficits. The city put up $45 million leaving an $80 million gap in annual funding. At a news conference Schweiker announced, "I believe we will give rise to the finest urban school system in the country." The agreement would mean that the schools would remain open with the new year. Schweiker's first move was to appoint James Nevels as the chair of a five-member panel to select an interim "CEO" for the system.

The governor's selection of Mr. Nevels was telling, because Mr. Nevels helped arrange for Edison to take control of the schools in Chester Upland's 6,800-student district this fall. Mr. Nevels, who appeared at the news conference, said he had been pleased with the company's performance in Chester Upland so far and would encourage his colleagues on the panel to give the company serious consideration.[13]

Following the agreement and the news conference, protesters declared their intention to keep fighting. "We want to keep our public schools public," one of the protesters, Carmella Shivers, 17, a junior at Philadelphia High School for Girls, said over a blare of horns. "We don't want to give money away that we could have for our own schools."[14]

On April 18, 2002, a school reform commission composed of three members appointed by Schweiker and two members by Street voted on transferring control of 42 schools, one of six schools in the city, to outside managers. Schweiker's appointees voted together for the plan that gave Edison 20 schools to run and gave for-profit Chancellor Beacon Academies five schools, nonprofit Foundations, Inc., four schools, Victory Schools, Inc., three schools, and Universal Companies (a new company started by record producer and musician Kenny Gamble) two schools. As well, Temple University received five schools and the University of Pennsylvania three. Although Edison received double the schools to run than it had in any single district, it was only a third of the 60 that it had expected. Edison stock dropped on news of the announcement. Wall Street analysts were not the only ones disappointed in the outcome.

> After the meeting, Jerry Jordan, a vice president of the Philadelphia Federation of Teachers, said he regretted that the panel had said so little about how the schools would be redesigned by the outsiders. "They didn't spell anything out," Mr. Jordan said. "It's like, 'Let's see what works.' It shows a total lack of respect." After the roll was called, several dozen student protesters, who have long argued that it was undemocratic for a for-profit company to operate a public school, chanted, "Shame!" and "I am not for sale!"[15]

With the beginning of the 2002–2003 school year, many articles appeared in newspapers suggesting that how Edison fared in Philadelphia would determine the fate of the company. *Business Week* wrote:

> Despite heavy spending this summer to open new schools, Edison still has $30 million in cash. "But this is their last

chance," says Trace Urdan, an analyst at ThinkEquity Partners, a boutique investment bank in San Francisco. By next June, Edison must pass its toughest exam yet — by proving that it can make money while effectively running schools in such tough places as Philadelphia. If it fails, Edison will likely either become a private company or face bankruptcy.[16]

At the beginning of Philly's first year with Edison, the Pennsylvania panel recruited former Chicago public schools "CEO" and failed Illinois Democratic primary gubernatorial candidate Paul Vallas to head the Philadelphia schools.

Vallas, an accountant by profession, was notorious for his embrace of quantified measures of achievement, disciplinary tactics, and especially for making students, teachers, and administrators compete against each other for scarce resources. Rather than leading Chicago teachers to lobby the city and state for more resources for a student population that is more than 90 percent below the poverty line and more than 90 percent non-white, the wealthy, white Vallas threatened Chicago teachers, undermined the teachers' unions, and used the competitive testing of students to force teachers to compete with each other to remain employed in their schools. Schools that did not improve their performance were "reconstituted." Essentially, teachers from schools with poor test scores were swapped with teachers from other schools with poor test scores. Continually poor test scores merited the hiring of "remediation specialists," who recommended the removal of teacher autonomy in the classroom through such remedies as scripted lessons, painstakingly broken-down lesson plans, the exhaustive elaboration of goals and objectives for every action, and dramatic increases in paperwork for teachers so that administrators could track and monitor such reform. According to Vallas' detractors, the results caused teachers to teach to the tests, promoted insecurity that was damaging to teacher morale, and undermined teaching as an intellectual activity.[17] Within Vallas' reforms, knowledge is thought of as unquestionable facts to drill into students or as a product to be delivered. In his letter to the U.S. Congressional Committee Hearings on Education and the Workforce, Vallas testified:

> To assist teachers in teaching to the standards, we have developed curriculum frameworks, programs of study, and curriculum models with daily lessons. These materials are based on training models designed by the Military Command and General Staff Council.

And while Vallas himself makes quite explicit that the model for his reforms are the military's training methods and his background in accounting, he does not address the role of such authoritarian methods in a democratic nation.

COMPETITION

The story of Edison in Philadelphia raises a number of questions about educational privatization and the ideal of competition. Privatizers invoke the ideal of competition as a way to suggest that the problems with public schools stem from bloated bureaucracy that allows students, teachers, and administrators to be complacent with the way things are. Grounded in a model of corporate governance, the competition thinking goes something like this: Lack of competition allows students to benefit from "social promotion" and have no fear of failing out; lack of competition allows teachers to remain protected by their teachers' union and thus have no fear of losing their jobs if their students do not learn; lack of competition with other schools allows administrators to be lax because they do not have to fear their resources being shifted to other schools that are improving. Notice that what all of these elements of the competition metaphor share is an emphasis on fear as the motivating factor in the behavior of everyone involved in public schools.

One very basic problem with this way of thinking is that what motivates students to learn, teachers to teach, and administrators to lead has little to do with such a negative motivator as fear. Rather, students ideally learn because they are intellectually curious about subjects; teachers ideally want to teach because they are concerned with helping their students develop self and social understanding as well as a capacity not only to negotiate the economy, but also to be engaged in private life in ways that are more fulfilling and to be engaged in public life in ways that further the goals of a substantive democracy. Administrators ideally want to help create the conditions where this is possible. Competition, like other market metaphors, misses the multiple public and private roles of public schooling beyond "delivery of information" for the participation of students in the national and global economies.

In Philadelphia, Edison trumpeted the virtues of competition but was quick to benefit from the largesse of a Republican state administration in avoiding competitive bidding on educational contracting. In fact, the governor's moves, first simply to hand over the schools to Edison and then, after retreating, to commission the very same company to study the situation, looked so suspicious to so many people that investigations were called for at the federal, state, and city levels.

Eyebrows should have been raised by the close connections between Republican politicos and Whittle dating back to the early 1990s.

> When he [Whittle] made speeches about for-profit education before various conferences of state governors in the early '90s, many implored him to take over their troubled public schools. His gubernatorial fans — largely Republican — included Lamar Alexander of Tennessee, Tom Ridge of Pennsylvania, and

George W. Bush of Texas. (William Weld, former governor of Massachusetts, later joined Edison's board.)[18]

These decade-old Republican connections were useful for Edison not only for Pennsylvania's seizure of Philly's schools for Edison, prepared for by Ridge, but also when it came time to investigate. The U.S. Department of Education under George W. Bush refused to investigate how Edison won its $60 million, five-year contract to manage those 20 schools. This came despite the dramatically increased role of the federal government in public schooling under the administration as characterized by the No Child Left Behind Act. Nonetheless, at the state level, Pennsylvania auditor general Robert P. Casey, Jr., found that the Pennsylvania Department of Education "violated its own competitive-bidding rules because it was 'hellbent' on awarding Edison Schools Inc. a $2.7 million 'sweetheart deal' to study the Philadelphia school district."[19]

According to F. Joseph Merlino, who independently examined Edison's contract, Edison "never adequately examined a set of interrelated problems that drove the district's crisis and led to its takeover."[20]

The state underfunds the district, he said, leaving city teachers underpaid, which drives a high turnover rate, which in turn contributes to poor student performance. "It was an outrageous sum of money to spend for inferior research," said Mr. Merlino, who trains city mathematics teachers through a grant program based at La Salle University in Philadelphia. "It was a document that justified a political takeover."[21]

Merlino and Casey's investigations reveal the extent to which resources were denied to Philadelphia by the state and then the state, in conjunction with Edison, accused the city of failing in its competition with the rest of the state to provide "quality" education.

Reliance on the magic of market competition to provide an adequate tax base to fund the schools resulted in Philadelphia's public schools being underfunded in the first place. Once the schools were devastated, market-based competition was trumpeted as the solution to the problems of public schooling. Philly was declared a basket case for failing to compete with other schools in Pennsylvania while no one in the state and few in mass media pointed to the reasons. The reasons include "an eroding tax base and a 1993 state freeze on school aid" that "drove multimillion-dollar deficits, ultimately precipitating Pennsylvania's takeover of the system in December."[22] This information from *U.S. News & World Report* offers another dimension to competition, one seldom raised in news reports about the situation in Philadelphia and elsewhere that Edison operates, namely, that by the time the private sector steps in promising to save beleaguered public schools with discipline-promoting competition and the corporate model, a whole lot of competition has already taken place. Competition between the private sector and the public for resources has been taking place. That eroding tax base in Philadelphia resulted from capital flight by corporations rushing to take their production to cheaper locales. And such a race to the bottom for cheap labor resulted in city and state governments competing against each other to lure corporations. The bait is tax incentives, tax rebates, cash, cash, and more public cash. And for what? Usually for low-paying jobs without benefits or security. For example, in Philadelphia at the end of the 1990s, Disney demanded a million dollars from the city and tax deferral to open a retail complex downtown. This was publicized as a great benefit for the city by bringing jobs when in reality the tax base was being depleted for the creation of a small number of mostly low-paying, minimum-wage jobs without benefits. The problem is not corrupt city officials so much as a structured race to the bottom as governments find themselves with depleted tax bases, desperate for money and competing against other localities for it.

The same neoliberal ideology that proposes that schooling be thought of as nothing but a business preaches the privatization of all public services and the end to barriers against trade. These different components of neoliberal ideology feed each other. When the local government has been impoverished by local industry going overseas, the neoliberals cry, "See! What these inefficient governments need is a little healthy dose of the free market! Privatize the services and hand them over to corporations to run for profit." Typically, this process is accompanied by a big dose of diatribe accusing nonwhite and working-class local residents of failing to care for their own community after they are victimized by the corporate dismemberment and state evisceration of their tax base. In short, a market-based model of competition in public schooling should hardly be accepted as a healthy way to think about the goals and values of public education. Furthermore, the only way to stop the race to the bottom is with a broad-based commitment to strengthening the public sector.

EDUCATIONAL PRIVATIZATION CANNOT COMPETE

The inability of Edison to compete with public schools has been a result not merely of poor management, alleged corruption, or bad luck. The failure of Edison to compete with the public schools has to do, in part, with the failures of educational privatization generally. The business press widely recognized this in the autumn of 2002. While *Business Week* declared Edison "the bellwether for the entire for-profit school-reform movement"[23] and pointed to the failures of Edison's financial model, *Fortune* came right out with the broader analysis that Edison is symptomatic of the industry. In an article titled, "Why Edison Doesn't Work," *Fortune* wrote:

Perhaps the simplest reason Edison doesn't work, though, is that for-profit education just isn't a very good business. Though a dozen or more competitors have sprung up in recent years — most much smaller than Edison — about the only profitable ones are $15.6 million Nobel Learning Communities, which runs mostly private schools, and National Heritage Academies, which runs 28 quasi-religious schools. For-profit schools are "low margin no matter how you slice it," says Steven Wilson, who started Advantage Schools in 1996. Economies of scale are almost nonexistent, says Columbia's Henry Levin, who heads the National Center for the Study of Privatization in Education at Columbia University's Teachers College. Then there's the quality of the Education. For-profit schools have to be orders of magnitude better than their public-school rivals in order to overcome the political opposition that confronts them. And so far that hasn't happened.[24]

While *Fortune* described educational privatization as bad business generally, it nonetheless identified a number of poor management decisions that Edison made. The first mistake was to bet on vouchers, which were never popular with middle-class suburbanites. (Vouchers are not quite dead yet. At the beginning of 2004 the U.S. Congress authorized the first federal voucher scheme in Washington, D.C.) The second mistake was the attempt to make Edison a growth company, which appeared to have the advantage of culminating in lower costs through volume down the road. However, according to *Fortune*, this was central to Edison's need for expensive capital and its willingness to incur unnecessary costs as well as its willingness to sign contracts that would allow school districts to break contracts and more importantly the willingness to offer services under costs simply to grow. By the end of 2002, Edison was $80 million in debt.[25]

Levin points to three basic strategies on the part of EMOs like Edison that are geared for cutting costs in order to provide the same or better services to students while still being able to skim profit off for investors: (1) hire less-experienced teachers; (2) standardize curriculum and operating procedures; (3) recruit and keep students who are "less demanding of resources, meaning fewer students with moderate to severe behavioral or learning needs."[26] According to Levin, most of what privatizers such as Edison claim to be doing as innovation is already present in most public schools. "Without question, there is no evidence of 'revolutionary' breakthroughs by EMOs with respect to curriculum, instructional strategies, or use of technologies."[27]

If for-profit education companies offer little evidence of being able to compete on grounds of quality, how about cost? According to educational experts such as Levin, the economies-of-scale logic that has been Whittle's central argument for eventually realizing profit will never work because although volume purchasing and model replication can reduce fixed costs, schools can never eliminate high variable costs. New schools will inevitably have new variable costs that will offset any benefit from economies of scale.

The inability of Edison to compete with public schools became even more evident when in 2003 Paul Vallas announced his intention to make Edison spend the same per pupil as students in other Philadelphia public schools receive. Vallas announced in May that he wanted to save $10 million in fees that the school system was paying to corporations and universities hired to run 45 schools. "The system's biggest and best-paid school management contractor, Edison Schools, would have its fees slashed by about $430 per-pupil under the proposal."[28] Vallas stated:

> Our general impression was that they [the firms] were overcompensated last year. If the argument is that private management

is superior to public management, and they can offer a better education for the same amount of money, great. But $800 to $900 more per-pupil is not the same amount of money.[29]

Edison was receiving "$881 more per-pupil than the administrators' budget for similar schools in the district."[30] Vallas was proposing not that the contractors receive the same amount that the public schools receive but $450 on top of what the public schools receive per student. But Vallas reported that when he met with state legislators:

It was clearly communicated to me that there would not be any support in Harrisburg for reducing the funding for these (firms) this year. I felt that if there was not going to be support for that, or if we were going to be circumvented ... then rather than run that risk, we would be willing to compromise with the understanding that we would have a commitment to get the help that we need to obviously implement the high school redesign.[31]

The high school redesign referred to a "compromise" deal that Vallas made with legislators for the district to receive $30 million for a high school improvement program that was proposed by the School Reform Commission that hired the privatization firms. The compromise included that the state would be willing "to work with the district on debt-free financing."[32] The School Reform Commission approved an operating budget for 2004 of $1.8 billion.

Steve Miskin, press secretary for House Speaker John Perzel, R-Philadelphia, said lawmakers, including Perzel and Dwight Evans, D-Philadelphia, believed that the firms needed more time before their funds were cut. "It's definitely the right thing to do to let them improve themselves," Miskin said.[33]

Although Vallas vowed to fire any management firm that did not perform up to expectations, as of the 2003–2004 school year, Edison continued to receive significantly higher per-pupil money from the state. The problem with this is not only that, as Vallas' above comments indicate, it flies in the face of the benefits of competition promised by advocates of privatization, but it also makes it impossible to judge the ability of Edison in comparison to the public schools that are not receiving this extra money. Finally, it is extremely difficult to see how the extra per-pupil expense footed by the Pennsylvania taxpayers is anything more than a gift to Edison's investors. If the schools need the extra per-pupil expense, then should it not go right into the school?

Vallas has advocated bringing in more "partners" for the Philadelphia schools. Vallas said he envisions that area universities will end up playing as big a role in managing city schools as for-profit firms like Edison Schools and Victory Schools, which were hired to run part of the district last summer. The district is also courting Philadelphia's science museum, The Franklin Institute, to become involved with its science curriculum. It has been in talks with area teaching hospitals and a health insurance company about opening an allied health academy. There's even an ongoing discussion with Microsoft about the software giant taking some sort of role in the school system, although officials have declined to discuss details.

Although press coverage of Vallas's demands on for-profits in Philadelphia played up a turn away from privatization, Vallas himself has made it clear that he does not categorically reject privatization.

"We support alternative management," Vallas said. "We just want to make sure it is the best alternative management." District officials insist they haven't abandoned the idea of hiring private firms specializing in school management to revitalize a school system plagued by poor test scores, crumbling facilities and violence. School reform Commission member James Gallagher said officials have simply expanded their idea of public–private partnerships to include arrangements in which the district might retain financial control of a school, but invite an institution like a university to handle academics. "What about corporations sponsoring high schools? What about hospitals, entrepreneurs, or community groups?" he asked. "We're all about inviting new parties to the public school party."[34]

The guest list at the public school party appears long and is getting longer, involving six universities and conservative former Secretary of Education William Bennett's Web-based company K12 that sells online for-profit charter school programs and homeschooling. In the summer of 2003, Vallas reported that the 16 schools that would be seeing outside involvement was "just the tip of the iceberg."[35]

Although Vallas stated that "few of the district's partners would be paid more than a few thousand dollars for their help," the partnership agreements will cost $3 million. St. Joseph's University will be paid nearly half a million dollars.[36] Several of the universities will use the schools as profit-generating laboratories to do teacher education and certification, thereby collecting tuition and student teaching fees without paying student teachers the salaries that would normally be paid to certified, experienced, and unionized teachers. The universities like it because their student teachers gain teaching experience while they collect money from students. The school district likes it because it can have universities associated with school reform initiatives and hence credibility. So who loses? For one thing, the schools are being shortchanged by not receiving the same kind of investment in experienced teachers that schools in wealthier districts receive. As well, these partnerships are experiments, meaning that there is not a guarantee of long-term stability for the schools. For example, Vallas fired Chancellor Beacon Academy for inferior services and now turns to completely untested companies such as the Web-based "virtual classroom" model of William Bennett's K12.[37]

LESSONS FROM PHILADELPHIA ABOUT COMPETITION

There are several points not to be missed here about Edison and competition:

(1) Competition between the public sector and the private sector: the corporate sector competes with the public sector for public money. This is evident not only in the state of Pennsylvania's seizure of the Philadelphia schools from the city. For example, the Bush Administration is pushing to shift control over the 38-year-old Head Start program from the federal level to the state level. This would enable a conservative administration that principally represents the interests of business to cut funding for the program while allowing conservative states to shift from nonprofit providers contracting with the federal government to private for-profit companies able to contract with states. The danger is in allowing states to shift preschool resources elsewhere and to merge the program into other programs, thereby weakening or dismantling Head Start's mission despite a proven record of success in serving a million three- to four-year-olds from low-income families by interweaving education with health, nutrition, and parental involvement (70 percent are nonwhite). The attack on Head Start is being partly justified on the basis that "performance-based testing" of these little kids would be a more "accountable" way of measuring the value of the program. This is a backdoor form of privatizating a government program, but it also reveals how battles between the public and private sectors are fought within the public sector. This policy of privatizing public services like education resembles other

initiatives to privatize government, like Medicare, pharmaceuticals for elderly people, pension funds, hospitals, social security, the digital airwave broadcast spectrum, to name but a few of the most newsworthy. The government, which should be composed of the public and should function for the public interest, is selling off the public's securities to large corporations even as it forces the public to bail out these same corporations by unknowingly investing its savings in their falling stocks. It is crucial to recognize that schools are not the only site where the public's goods are being pillaged.

(2) Competition between the public and private sectors is deeply influenced by the competition for the representation of the world. Writing in *The New York Times* on the state's turnaround on Edison's management of the Philadelphia schools, Jacques Steinberg concludes his article with a quote from a parent: "'We are the consumers,' Pat Raymond, a parent leader, told a gathering of parents, students and others at Northeast High School after the decision was announced. 'Parents must demand to be heard.'"[38] Although Steinberg notes the continuing dissatisfaction with the state takeover and the undermining of local control and authority, he does not comment on the problem of some of the opposition to for-profit schooling adopting the market language of consumer satisfaction with educational provision. Once citizens accept the redefinition of public schooling as a consumer good, privatization appears as natural and universal public provision is no longer taken for granted as the baseline assumption. *The New York Times, The Boston Globe, The San Francisco Chronicle,* and *The Philadelphia Inquirer* all gave Edison generally favorable coverage and for the most part they did not challenge or question the premises that underlie for-profit schooling, including the basic one that public schooling is like a private service. The way that corporate media largely represent events in the interests of business rather than in the public interest is hardly restricted to newspapers or to coverage of public schooling.[39]

(3) Competition within the public sector: Different sections and constituencies of a state compete against each other for public resources. Despite common conservative accusations of "class warfare" when liberals suggest that the wealthiest citizens should pay their fair share, class warfare is exactly what goes on in the struggle over educational resources as illustrated by Edison, the battle over Head Start, and countless other examples. It was well understood by predominantly wealthy, predominantly white lawmakers in Harrisburg that the 1993 Pennsylvania state freeze on school aid would not cripple the schooling in rich, largely white places such as Lower Marion County that borders Philadelphia. The competition over the Philadelphia schools was not only between supporters of public education and supporters of market models of schooling, it was also between a largely white state government and a largely black city government and school system. Nonwhite students constitute nearly 75 percent of the Philadelphia student population. Philadelphia: African American 65.8 percent; white 15.6 percent; Hispanic 13.4 percent; Asian 5.1 percent; native American 0.2 percent.[40] This "minority" representation is roughly the opposite that of most of the state. Recall the above quote about why white Republicans did not want to embrace Ridge's voucher schemes:

> The unpleasant secret is that some in our party oppose vouchers because they don't want poor children from the inner city coming into their neighborhoods to go to school.[41]

This quote makes clear that "some" white advocates of privatization stop the push for privatization when it stands to integrate public schools racially. The privatization debates are thoroughly interwoven with race. Advocates of privatization rely heavily on the media-distributed imagery of corporate multiculturalism. Think of all the bank commercials that show an interracial crowd of professionals smiling in business suits. Although the corporate sector has become significantly more racially integrated than in its lily-white not too distant past, the promise of corporate multiracial integration is an illusion not only because of how few jobs are offered to nonwhites by the corporate sector,[42] but also because wage inequalities are worsening rather than improving. For example, in 1979 African American women earned 93 percent of whites whereas in 1998 they earned 84 percent of whites. African American men earned 76 percent of whites in 1979 and this did not change. Latinas earned 83 percent of whites in 1979, whereas in 1998 they earned 70 percent of whites. Latinos in 1979 earned 74 pecent of whites, whereas in 1998 they earned 63 percent of whites.[43] The cutting of social services and the downward pressure on wages resulting from capital flight has most adversely affected nonwhite workers. The selling of public school privatization through its association with TV images of a diverse corporate workforce stands starkly at odds with these economic trends.

LEAVING CHILDREN BEHIND IN THE COMPETITION FOR CONTRACTED REMEDIATION

The Pennsylvania seizure of the Philadelphia schools that served as a precursor to privatization initiatives can be viewed as a model for the way the federal government has treated states and locales through the No Child Left Behind legislation. Both the Philadelphia situation and No Child Left Behind reveal that, despite claims about the efficiency-producing wonders of competition touted by privatization advocates, privatization initiatives are being driven by government setups designed to benefit education companies. Governor Ridge's and Governor Schweiker's convictions that local democratic control was to blame for problems in Philadelphia and that state authority should be used to allow the private sector to experiment with urban schooling was a conviction shared by the George W. Bush Administration.

> The notion that new managers can significantly improve student achievement lies at the heart of President Bush's school reform package [No Child Left Behind]. A key element of that plan, now [November 6, 2001] inching its way through a congressional conference committee, calls for persistently failing schools to be given new staffs, converted to charter schools or run by private managers.[44]

No Child Left Behind makes states create performance-based achievement measures that must be met within a specific time frame. When those goals are not met, states will be required to spend public money on remediation. Much of this will be a boon for private for-profit test companies, educational publishers, and for-profit consulting companies.

As Stephen Metcalfe has shown, the "scientific" standards of No Child Left Behind were created by the same companies, such as McGraw-Hill, lined up to do remediation. Remediation by test companies and educational publishers means that this "accountability"-based reform was in large part set up as a way for these testing and publishing companies to profit by getting federally mandated and state-mandated business. The ideal of competition driving school reform could not be farther from the state and corporate practice of setting up a command economy through crony capitalism.

> The Bush legislation has ardent supporters in the testing and textbook publishing industries. Only days after the 2000 election, an executive for publishing giant NCS Pearson addressed a Waldorf ballroom filled with Wall Street analysts. According to *Education Week*, the executive displayed a quote from President-elect Bush calling for state testing and school-by-school report cards, and announced, "This almost reads like our business plan."[45]

The market ideal of competition driving testing-based reform could not be farther from the lack of market competition in the state and corporate practice of setting up these reforms through the kind of crony capitalism Metcalfe details. These ever more frequent tests that largely measure socially valued knowledge and cultural capital[46] (most of which students learn at home and in their social class milieu) will be used to justify remediation by states and locales, which will rely heavily on for-profit contractors. The federal government will insist that test scores be improved either (1) by allowing students to go to other schools or (2) by using public money for remediation efforts. The courts have already determined that the federal government will not enforce at the local level the freedom of students to go to better schools. So the remediation route is likely to be the biggest result of No Child Left Behind. Bush's No Child policy has led to increasing corporate management of curricula and standardized testing. This has become an excuse to close down public schools and an opening for the school privatization movement in remediation. As Metcalfe makes clear, most of the reforms tied to No Child Left Behind do not foster a culture that makes questioning power central. Rather, it deepens and expands authoritarian values, counters teaching as an intellectual endeavor, and by standardizing curriculum and employing discipline-based remediation, it simultaneously inhibits the critical engagement with knowledge and turns to the corporate sector to use tests, scripts, and prepackaged curriculum to drill knowledge into kids.

As many critics have suggested, No Child Left Behind has succeeded where voucher schemes have failed to garner public support for privatizing schools.[47] While massive evidence existed from the experiments of the 1970s regarding the failures of educational privatization,[48] nonetheless within the market triumphalism of the 1990s and the ascendancy of neoliberal ideology,

privatizing schools, according to the press and right-wing educational policy hounds, just had not been given the chance it
deserved. The failure of for-profits to make money and the
continuing unpopularity with voucher schemes, especially
among privileged segments of the population who already benefit from some of the best public schools in the world, have
resulted in a growing consensus that voucher schemes are not
feasible as a large-scale project. However, No Child Left Behind
brings privatization through the back door by setting up schools
for enforced private remediation. For example, now that Edison
has failed to compete at raising test scores, running schools
better than public schools, competing with other local public
schools, or keeping communities happy, it has launched Edison
Affiliates, a consulting firm focusing on administrative reform
and test score improvement. Edison Affiliates, which is going
by the name Tungten Learning, is likely to benefit from yet more
Republican largesse in the form of No Child Left Behind as it
appeals to the linkage of federal funding to test improvement
and lends itself to private remediation to do so.

No Child Left Behind also attempts to bring privatization
through the back door by forcing school districts to allow
students to leave "failing" schools to attend better ones. This
latter scheme, in part through massive federal support for for-
profit charter school development, aims to encourage vouchers.
It is important to note that this scheme, which theoretically
allows poor students to attend rich schools and nonwhite students to attend white schools, is not being enforced by the
federal government. As a result, the real effect will likely be that
second-rate for-profit charter schools will be the only viable
alternative for poor students and nonwhite students to leave
their "failing" schools. What is most important in all of this is
that the federal initiatives are not designed to invest in public
schools and communities that have been historically underresourced. Rather, the federal initiatives are designed to demand

improvement without adequate resource improvement and then to allow private companies to profit from public money on the promise of remedying the situation after the communities have been denied that opportunity.

The issue about competition here is not simply that communities are being denied the resources to compete with other communities for quality schooling, but also that the very way of thinking about quality schooling through competition is at odds with a democratic ideal of developing a critical citizenry capable of self-governance and deliberation about the future of the community and the nation. The current mode of educational reform designed around enforcement of standards from "above" and profit-driven remediation aims to squelch this possibility of the public democratic promise of schooling, thereby keeping students from developing the skills and abilities they need to share in educated decision-making about the future.

5

CORPORATE SCHOOLING AND THE FUTURE OF THE PUBLIC

On September 12, 2001, as smoke billowed from ground zero and televisions continued to flicker with the looped images of the collapsing twin towers, most Americans felt a tremendous desire to do something for others, to help the victims and their families, to contribute to the public. Americans from all over the nation went to New York City to do whatever they could from the treacherous work of putting out the fire at the World Trade Center to digging debris to donating blood to supplying rescue workers with food to just being there to cheer for those heroically going to the wreckage or returning from it with remains. The money that citizens sent, the tributes they erected, the flags they flew, and the conversations they had were part of an outpouring of public sentiment. On September 12, something opened up.

The standard cynicism and distrust about the motives of others and the cheap commercialism insisting that we are foremost consumers of toothpaste and beer briefly fell away. It was not just that we got a respite from the regular dose of TV ads and shows insisting that we live in a community of pathological strangers and violent criminals, of trivial people spouting inanities to an idiotic, laugh-track public. A break from a TV world of strangers trying to take something from you, take your money or your life, a media world made insecure by other people and a world made secure and comforting by promising personal possession, insularity from others. The corporate cult of Me, the security, predictability, and regularity of my McDonald's, my computer, of my personal pan pizza briefly broke. On September 12 people in public spaces, on subways, and in the street looked into each other's eyes, the eyes of strangers, and they thought, "That could have been me and that could have been you, and that shouldn't be anybody."

And people wanted to give something to others. They wanted to give with no expectation of return. Makeshift public institutions were created in lower Manhattan. On Chelsea Pier a hospital was made. Memorials to the missing were erected in the streets with paper and wood and wire and the streets were chalked. Someone wrote the word "Love" on the asphalt. What briefly opened up was a public spirit of generosity, a desire to help others, and a desire to understand. Out of tremendous tragedy, tremendous opportunity opened up for citizens to rethink the values of American life. This was an opportunity for so many to evaluate not only what they desire and value in daily life, but also how all Americans are treated and maybe even how all people on the planet are treated. Many Americans began wondering in public and in private why, if we could come together as a national community for the victims of September 11, we could not come together for others among us who suffer:

the homeless, the poor, those without health care, and children who make up the majority of those Americans living in dire poverty. If we could set up public institutions like that hospital on Chelsea Pier why can't we do this around the nation? Why not around the world? And why stop with public health? Why not public education? A beautiful, hopeful infection of generous sentiment began to spread. A desire was rekindled, a distinctly public desire, to heroically and patriotically give of oneself for the benefit of others. And then came the backlash.

First New York City mayor Rudolph Giuliani and then President Bush appeared on television and told Americans that the most patriotic thing that Americans could do was go to the malls and go shopping. It was made quite clear by the corporate-primed leaders of the public sector that the role of citizens was not the public role of participating in whatever should be done next, but the private role of consuming. At the same time corporate media began increasingly focusing their attention away from the vast generosity of the public and instead emphasized incidents of September 11 donor fraud, problems with the Red Cross, and assailed those who dared to ask whether the U.S. government's historical actions in the name of democracy had anything to do with what happened. The fever of generosity was successfully reshaped into war fever.

The War on Terrorism was announced as a new national condition, with no foreseeable end, a seemingly permanent war like the Cold War. Unlike the Cold War, this war would have no clearly defined enemy and no clearly defined ideological opponent. Militant Islamist organizations were interchangeable with secular Arab states, which were interchangeable with Islamist states, which were interchangeable with Stalinist regimes such as North Korea. President Bush made the dividing line in absolute terms that would brook no dissent or discussion: "You are either for us, or against us." The commercials returned and with them an unprecedented wave of propaganda rallying for war, the reformulation of U.S. foreign policy to indefinitely maintain American economic and military superiority by attacking any country that could possibly in the future become powerful enough to challenge the U. S., and the passage of the U.S. Patriot Act, which severely limited civil liberties. Not only was the role of the citizen declared by the government and the private sector to be principally the private role of going shopping, but the privacy guaranteed in private life by the Bill of Rights was no longer safe.

These attacks on democratic public life expanded the power of the state and corporate sector in a number of ways. In what follows here, I discuss the ways that expanded corporate control over politics, economy, and culture threatens the promises of American democracy and how the case of Edison Schools should be understood more as a symptom of the much larger threats posed to democratic public life than as a limited issue with student test scores or the effective delivery of educational services.

EDISON AS A SYMPTOM OF NEOLIBERALISM

The Rise and Fall of the Edison schools is not merely a story about the experiment with privatization as one educational reform experiment. The idea of privatizing a public service such as education is a relatively recent phenomenon that characterizes the broader social movement known as neoliberalism. Despite the misleading name, neoliberalism is in fact a form of conservatism, radical fiscal conservatism. Neoliberalism, which has its origins with the economists Frederick Hayek and Milton Friedman, suggests that markets can be trusted to resolve economic and social problems. As a corollary, the failure to embrace markets fully enough explains economic and social problems. Within this perspective, the role of the social welfare and caregiving parts of the public sector should be minimized and the private sector should be allowed to do its magic. Public services should be privatized and trade should be unfettered by tariffs and other barriers designed to protect markets. What is radical about neoliberalism is its hostility to public sector programs and its faith in markets to "naturally" accomplish social goals with the minimum of public planning. As eminent sociologist Pierre Bourdieu explained, neoliberalism does not merely defund the care-giving functions of the state, but rather shifts investment from the care-giving functions of the state to the punitive and repressive functions of the state, police and military, that enforce the neoliberal order domestically and internationally.

The economic and political doctrine of neoliberalism insists on the virtues of privatization and liberalization of trade and concomitantly places faith in the hard discipline of the market for the resolution of all social and individual problems. Within the United States, neoliberal policies have been characterized by their supporters as, "free market policies that encourage private enterprise and consumer choice, reward personal responsibility and entrepreneurial initiative, and undermine the dead hand of the incompetent, bureaucratic and parasitic government, that can never do good even if well intended, which it rarely is." [1] Within the neoliberal view, the public sphere should either be privatized as in the call to privatize U.S. public schools, public parks, social security, health care, etc., or the public sphere should be in the service of the private sphere as in the case of U.S. federal subsidies for corporate agriculture, entertainment, and defense,[2] as well as the vast array of "wealthfare" transfers of public money to the wealthiest citizens through tax laws, tax credits, industry subsidies and corporate bailouts, resource handouts, that were estimated by 1996 to be worth $448 billion.[3] This figure precedes the George W. Bush trillion-dollar tax cuts for the richest Americans.

The Clinton Administration embraced neoliberalism by pursuing international trade agreements that would benefit the corporate sector globally. Domestically, Clinton fostered such neoliberal reforms as the corporate takeover of health care in the form of the HMO, the end of welfare protections, and the implementation of Workfare to insist that everyone prove himself or herself "productive." Ultimately, these policies have proved disastrous for the most vulnerable citizens. For example, more than forty million Americans have no health insurance and minimum wage and union protection was undermined by those forced into workfare.

Under the Bush Administration, the faith in the market is even more radical. As Thomas Frank, Bill Moyers, and a number of other critics have suggested, the real aim of the massive tax cuts of the Bush Administration has been to demolish the last vestiges of social spending in the United States by putting the nation into massive debt. Over 10 years, these trillion-dollar tax cuts on corporate tax dividends and upper income brackets will marginally benefit the wealthiest Americans, while threatening the very survival of the poorest and intensifying reliance on the private sector to respond in ways that will only benefit the wealthiest even more.

This hostility to all things public under the George W. Bush Administration is exemplified by the statements of the leading Republican strategist Grover Norquist. Bill Moyers eloquently captures the broader goals of these fiscal conservatives:

> Their stated and open aim is to change how America is governed — to strip from government all its functions except those that reward their rich and privileged benefactors. They are quite candid about it, even acknowledging their mean spirit in accomplishing it. Their leading strategist in Washington — the same Grover Norquist — has famously said he wants to shrink the government down to the size that it could be drowned in a bathtub. More recently, in commenting on the fiscal crisis in the states and its affect on schools and poor people, Norquist said, "I hope one of them" — one of the states — "goes

bankrupt." So much for compassionate conservatism. But at least Norquist says what he means and means what he says. The White House pursues the same homicidal dream without saying so. Instead of shrinking down the government, they're filling the bathtub with so much debt that it floods the house, water-logs the economy, and washes away services for decades that have lifted millions of Americans out of destitution and into the middle-class. And what happens once the public's property has been flooded? Privatize it. Sell it at a discounted rate to the corporations.[4]

Neoliberalism is the dominant ideology of the present moment but also the one most affecting schooling at every level.

The central aspects of neoliberalism in U.S. education involve three intertwined phenomena: (1) structural transformations in terms of funding and resource allocations: the privatization of public schools including voucher schemes, for-profit charter schools, and school commercialism initiatives; (2) the framing of educational policy reform debates and public discourse about education in market terms rather than public terms. The intensified corporate control over meaning-making technologies generally has played a large part in reshaping the public discussion about education. Both corporate control over mass media and its increasing role in schooling have been central to imagining of schooling as a market; and (3) the ideology of corporate culture in schools that imagines the school as ideally being recreated to model the corporation.

In neoliberal ideology, the individual is conceived privately in economic terms as a consumer or worker rather than publicly and politically as a citizen. The dismantling of Aid for Families with Dependent Children and the creation of Workfare programs initiated under the Clinton Administration in fact illustrate these twin demands as they are imposed on citizens: welfare programs represent investment in unproductive individuals with no return on investment while the most important aspect of Workfare is less about financial saving for the state than it is about making "productive individuals" through the wielding of coercive state power. While the ideological dimension of this reform may trump the financial, it is important not to lose sight of the way that within neoliberalism the coercive and punitive functions of the state are bolstered while the care-giving functions of the state are dismantled. As Pierre Boudieu suggested, neoliberalism is in this way highly gendered by attacking those institutions such as welfare, education, and health care traditionally associated with femininity and strengthening those institutions traditionally associated with masculinity such as military, policing, incarceration, and criminal justice.[5]

In the case of Edison this disciplinary tendency of neoliberal ideology becomes readily apparent in a number of ways. Edison relies heavily on ideas of the disciplined corporation that remedies the lack of discipline in a female teacher workforce and the lack of discipline in a nonwhite student body. As discussed in Chapter Three, Edison and other EMOs appear as the deliverer of fiscal discipline in schools and communities that are consistently accused in mass media and educational policy of suffering principally not from unjust resource allocation to schools and communities and not from the unjust application of cultural value but rather from being populated with undisciplined individuals — teachers who do not work hard enough, teachers who do not follow the prescribed curriculum, students who do not work hard enough, students who do not follow the rules of conduct. Educational privatizers merge the metaphor of fiscal discipline with the metaphor of physical discipline. Students who refuse to pay attention, teachers who refuse to follow the prescribed curriculum, according to the disciplinary ideals of neoliberal ideology — these are out-of-control bodies in need of enforcement-oriented reforms. Domestic militarization and zero-tolerance policies enforce neoliberal visions for schooling that

of September 11 was the passage of the Bush Administration military budget of over $400 billion a year (not including the war on Iraq) of which only 10 to 15 percent was tied to increased security against terrorism.[7] This record level of military spending[8] not only exceeds that of the rest of the industrialized countries combined, but it also constitutes a truly massive transfer of public money to high-tech corporations. The results are not only increased weapons dealing by the United States, which destabilizes regions by creating regional arms races, but also the squandering of the potential to transform this nation through domestic social spending, to fulfill every citizen's needs for education, health care, and housing, and to invest in the same provisions in nations that see nothing from the United States but shrapnel, bomblets, and bullets.[9] The implications of such backward policies and priorities are that democratic participation domestically is deterred by keeping the population in scarcity and miseducation. As well, these policies endanger the American public with U.S. foreign policy that terrorizes other nations,[10] thereby producing terrorism while also terrorizing segments of the population at home through racist policing, record levels of incarceration and sentencing, the militarization of civil society in the form of the militarizing of the local police, the U.S. military taking on police functions, and the police spying on the population in the name of national security.[11] The "War on Terror" has been a boon for justifying intensified privatization as Bechtel privatizes schools in Iraq, Haliburton makes billions on rebuilding, and private mercenary firms constitute more than ten percent of troops in Iraq — a war that will likely benefit oil companies after the rebuilding profits have been made.[12] As Naomi Klein and Christian Parenti argue the Iraqi resistance to U.S. occupation is as much about who will control national resources and industry as it is about political autonomy. The invasion may have been one of the grandest uses of force to transform Iraq on the neoliberal model. While public goods and services are increasingly subject to privatization fever, corporate risk is being socialized.

Neoliberal deregulation allowed Enron to exist by speculating on energy markets without essentially producing anything. Then, its spectacular implosion was framed in corporate media not as symptomatic of the fundamental problem with turning public utilities over to the private sector (a fact that California's blackout situation should have suggested) but as a matter of accounting irregularities. Public bailout on this one? Billions. The fact that the Bush Administration is stacked with former energy executives and was taking policy directives from Enron right to the end points to more than a high level of corruption among an indignantly righteous cabal of martially minded moral crusaders. It highlights the extent to which the political process and its representation have been hijacked by the corporate sector. The corporatization of education including the Edison case needs to be understood in relation to the ways that the meaning of democracy have been successfully transformed by fiscal elites and skillfully repackaged as little more than the growth of the corporate controlled economy. Returning to September 12, 2001 when Mayor Giuliani and President Bush exhorted the public that the way to be patriotic was to go shopping, this was indicative that the very notion of the public as a means of assuring the collective good is in peril of eradication as the role of the public sector aside from transferring wealth to corporations is reduced to its coercive functions of military and policing. Concomitant with attacks on the public, privacy is under attack.

As private conversations invade public space through cell phone use, reality television expands the talk show format that makes petty gossip and private concerns with bedroom and bathroom behavior into matters of national concern. The "War on Terror" has allowed conservatives to seize on an opportunity to drastically reduce civil liberties such as rights to privacy. These invasions of privacy work in conjunction with the attacks on the public sphere because public participation, which is the essence of democracy, requires of individuals knowledge about issues of public import, reflection, as well as the capacity to identify with public concerns. Corporate media have been succeeding spectacularly at not only inundating the public arena with information of no public import, but also inducing identifications with principally private matters such as personal safety, individual morality, health, and sex, the ordering and regulating of the body and interpersonal relationships. The making of public concerns such as economic security and political participation into personal matters undermines the collective and individual capacity to act to transform the conditions that produce public and individual problems. What is necessary is the creation of pedagogies that translate individual concerns back into matters of public deliberation. To address the kinds of threats individuals face will require the kind of public collective action that corporate media expunges from its representational universe. As such, cultural politics — the struggle over meanings — is an essential aspect of a progressive democratic practice inside and outside of classrooms. As the second chapter illustrated, Edison's design and curriculum are hostile to the healthy encouragement of the struggle over meanings essential to public institutions in a democratic society. The kinds of educational change necessary to make a thoughtful, critical public will require public schools that do not just deliver information, that focus not just on skills and facts and not even just on problem-solving skills, but on what Paulo Freire called education as the practice of freedom that encourages an understanding that learning and teaching are interventions in the world. While public schools are far from a widespread embrace of democratic approaches to education, we can be certain that corporate schooling and the undermining of public schooling will threaten to inhibit the development of forms of education that can address the most pressing public problems of the day.

Enforcement of standards, standardization, performance-based assessment, school reconstitution, high-stakes testing, zero tolerance, uniforms, the Troops to Teachers program — all such programs and reforms aim for the enforcement of the "right" knowledge and methods and all but eclipse traditional roles of public schools including civic education, the making of the whole person, or other socially transformative justifications for schooling, let alone the progressive ideals of taking up knowledge in relation to power and making critical education part of a broader project for social transformation. I have referred elsewhere to this phenomenon as "Education as Enforcement." "Education as Enforcement" understands militarized public schooling as part of the militarization of civil society. This in turn needs to be understood as part of the broader social, cultural, and economic movement for corporate globalization that seeks to erode public democratic power and expand and enforce corporate power locally, nationally, and globally. Ellen Meiskins Wood calls corporate globalization "the New Imperialism" that seeks to control markets everywhere and all the time.[13] In this sense the Bush Administration's new doctrine of permanent war is a more overt expression of corporate globalization, which should be viewed as a doctrine that is driven by the ideology of neoliberalism.

What keeps the U.S. public supporting or at least assenting to the misuse of public funds and the marginalization of the public from decision making about the future of work, consumption, the fate of nature, and leisure among other values that concern everybody is not principally the $400 billion a year arsenal. It is education, broadly conceived, that teaches individuals what to believe and value and how to understand themselves in relation to others — that teaches the range of possible futures that can be imagined. But if education is involved in holding people in place, it also offers the capacity for imagining new and different individual and collective futures, rethinking the relations between self and other, and formulating new language to describe and transform the world.

The repressive elements of the state in the form of such phenomena as the suspension of civil liberties under the U.S. Patriot Act, militarized policing, the radical growth of the prison system, and intensified surveillance accompany the increasing corporate control of daily life. The corporatization of the everyday is characterized by the corporate domination of information production and distribution in the form of control over mass media and educational publishing, the corporate use of information technologies in the form of consumer identity profiling by marketing and credit card companies, and the increasing corporate involvement in public schooling and higher education at multiple levels.

It is utterly imperative that educators and others grasp that the corporate takeovers in education are only part of the increasing corporate control over health care, military, agriculture, information, and the political process. The key issue is the shift of political power at every level of social life and everywhere on the planet, which is not only undermining democratic political power, but is also spreading the corporate management of everyday life through knowledge production in conjunction with military/police coercion. With the reformulation of strategic doctrine (the National Security Strategy) the U.S. government has now declared it will wage preventive war on any potential rivals for U.S. military or economic hegemony. This is hardly about expanding the will of the people either in the United States or abroad and very much about expanding the profit of corporations by killing those abroad who would conceivably stifle expanded corporate control of local economies and by enforcing the economic dictates of U.S.-led international financial entities.

Teachers have a moral responsibility to challenge abusive corporate–state power inside and outside the classroom in the name of human rights and a political responsibility to challenge it in the name of genuine democracy. To fail in this regard is to be complicit with the demise of the conditions necessary for a truly democratic nation and to fail in this regard is to be complicit with the rush to atrocity here and abroad. One of the great threats to the expansion of democracy in America is corporations such as Edison privatizing public schools and thereby limiting the public forums for citizens to learn about, debate, and challenge the radical amassing of political power, cultural power, and economic power by few citizens.

DEFENDING PUBLIC SCHOOLS: BEYOND THE BATTLE OVER COMMERCIALISM

Activists and writers have been making spectacular inroads against school commercialism. For example, a number of school districts across the nation have rejected soft drink vending contracts and advertising in their schools. Commercialism is the most obvious facet of corporate involvement in schools and one that most citizens find appalling at a commonsense level. The making of classrooms into places where students are bombarded with ads in the curriculum, on "educational" television "news" programs, suggests the destruction of schooling as a place safe from the normal barrage of incessant sell jobs that are nearly omnipresent in the culture from highway billboards to hypermarketing in stores, to the ubiquitous television, to the heavy ad content of most print material such as magazines that citizens come in contact with on a daily basis. But one of the greatest possibilities of public school classrooms is their capacity to be places where students learn the knowledge and tools to comprehend and criticize social injustices and to develop capacities to imagine and enact a better world together with other citizens. The corporate vision for the future imagines students as developing as workers and consumers but is, in reality, hostile to students developing their capacities for civic engagement ultimately to participate publicly in making society. What kinds of social, political, and ethical visions do corporations have and how are these visions related to their plans for schools? How about citizens collectively committed to making a more democratic, equal, and just society — how are these visions related to their plans for schools?

Critics of Edison and other corporations aiming to make inroads into public schooling can benefit from the insights of Bowles and Gintis's *Schooling in Capitalist America*, which powerfully challenges the assumptions that both liberals and many conservatives bring to the criticism of school commercialism: namely, that commercialism threatens an abstract notion of "quality education" that the school offers without the interference of business.

Bowles and Gintis remind us that schools largely function to discipline the future adult population for its participation (or nonparticipation) in the labor force and political system; that social control is accomplished in part through the internalization of behavioral norms inculcated by schools; that the grading system is the most basic process of rewarding conformity to the social order of the school; that students are rewarded for compliance and submission to authority, which is at odds with personal growth and democratic participation; that the hidden and overt curriculum of the school plays a central role of depoliticizing class relations of the production process; that economic inequality and personal development are primarily defined by the market, by property, and by power relations that define a capitalist economy; and that racial and gender/sex identification is interwoven with the formation of hierarchy of authority and status in the process. In short, the corporate entry into schools is not brand-new and it runs far deeper than the introduction of advertising and product placement in curriculum, deeper than for-profit public schooling.

The deep structural ways that schools function in the interests of capital complicates the aforementioned commonsense revulsion that most people feel about school commercialism — a common sense echoed in liberal educational policy circles that presume that everyone knows what is wrong with business getting into schools. That is, it threatens some abstract notion of a "quality" education. However, many practical and well-meaning liberals do not want to address what "quality" means. As a result the question of the underlying function of schools is evaded. Instead of facing the reality that schools largely reproduce relations of production and undermine democratic participation, liberals and conservatives affirm the dominant vision for schools, one defined through individual upward economic mobility and global economic competition.

This is a really important point and needs to be remembered as so many articles appear from a liberal perspective in scholarly press from the perspective of efficacy (accepting reforms such as performance-based assessment, high-stakes testing, etc.) without considering how such reforms participate in enacting business's vision for the future. The point is also utterly essential to recognize, considering the inroads that the corporate sector has made in legitimating businesspeople as educational policy spokespersons. The embrace of this "whatever works" mentality aids the private sector in capturing public schools to serve the interests of the private accumulation of capital at the expense of kids and broader social ideals. This owes largely to the ways that educational language has overtaken the field, undermining the public language and referents for thinking about schools.

Unfortunately, disparities in wealth and income have consistently worsened since the 1970s, expanding communities beset by poverty. Consider the following facts and figures available with full citation at www.inequality.org:

- Since the mid-1970s, the most fortunate 1 percent of households has doubled its share of the national wealth. The top 1 percent now holds more wealth than the bottom 90 percent of the population.
- In 2001, 16.3 percent of American children lived in poverty, a lower rate than 1993 (22.7 percent), but higher than the 1973 rate of 14.4 percent.
- Between 1983 and 1998, households in the bottom 20 percent of the population saw their net worth decline from − $3,200 to − $8,900 in 1998 dollars. Meanwhile, the net worth of the middle fifth of the population rose 3.7 percent, and the net worth of the top 1 percent rose 30 percent.
- In 1998, the typical black household held only 12 percent of the wealth of the typical white household. With housing excluded, that figure would be 3 percent. More than 27 percent of black households (and nearly 15 percent of white households) have no net worth.
- As of 1998, 48 percent of American households owned stock either directly or through a mutual fund or some sort of retirement plan. More than 86 percent of the value of all stocks and mutual funds, including pensions, was held by the top 10 percent of the households.

These inequalities could be one reason the promise of the Edison schools to do what public schools in poor communities could not do seems so alluring — particularly for those citizens historically short-changed by the public school resource allocations that have been tied to local property wealth and a legacy of racialized economic privilege. The right-wing investment in marketing privatization to African Americans and other non-white communities has played up the historical failure of the public school system to provide universally, suggesting that it is time to "give the market a chance." One problem with such thinking is that it obscures the causes for the historically unequal distribution of educational resources in the first place.

Much of the reason for the success of privatizers in marketing education to working-class and poor minorities has involved the successful redefinition of schooling as a consumer choice. Within this marketized social vision, privatized schooling appears as an increase in local control and autonomy, although defined through consumption rather than universal access to public services for all citizens. The appearance of increased local control comes despite the reality that control shifts to wherever the corporate headquarters are. San Francisco's Edison Charter Academy reports to Edison headquarters in New York City while its contract is with the State of California in Sacramento. Privatized schooling also appeals through its association with the elite private consuming choices of the wealthy. Finally, privatized schooling appeals to populations disenchanted with the historical failure of the state to provide quality universal schooling. When politicians advocating privatization say, "give the market a chance," some minority, working-class, and poor constituents buy into the market myth that, unlike the state, the only color of the market is green. Sadly, what the privatizers marketing for-profit schooling fail to mention is that historically the school choice movement has racist origins in maintaining racial segregation in public schools.[14] Moreover, in the words of Makani N. Themba:

> The conservatives pushing school vouchers [and by extension we can add for-profit charter schools] are not committed to fighting for better schools for all. They are seeking to pull much-needed resources out of public schools and funnel the money

into private schools. Fundamentally, they are looking for new ways for whites to maintain segregation and privilege. (Nationwide, 78 percent of private school students are white; 9 percent are African American and 8 percent are Latino.)[15]

It is essential to recognize that the above-mentioned economic inequalities and legacies of racial injustice cannot be solved with school reform alone. To address long-standing social injustices requires transforming communities through public and private investment, job availability, and social safety nets. Just working to improve schools alone does not get at the reasons poor communities have few to no jobs, have expensive check-cashing stands instead of banks, have expensive convenience stores but no grocery stores, have disproportionate levels of pollution and asthma rates, have inferior public parks, little to no public health facilities, and have higher levels of disease, violent crime, alcoholism, and drug abuse that consistently arise from such devastating conditions and the psychological toll it takes on individuals. The same conditions that produce cynicism and despair about the future in poor communities produce cynicism about political participation to remedy such social problems.

The structural analysis typified by Bowles and Gintis undermines the fiction of the innocence of the school as a space outside the relations of capital that only becomes tainted with the most explicit entry of business, like advertising in textbooks. Noted education writer Alfie Kohn has argued recently that the factory model is alive and well.[16] I would agree and then add that one of the important tasks for critics of corporatization to comprehend now is how the reproduction of the conditions of production is shifting from an industrial to a service model in some places and in others shifting from an industrial to a prison/military model. This means that privileged, largely white schools are being remade on the model of corporate culture with the goal of training future managers and consumers in a service economy while the public schools serving economically redundant working-class and poor segments of the population are increasingly given discipline in schools.

The meritocratic ideal that structures educational discourse and policy debate is both itself an example of capitalist ideology structuring schools and a gross distortion of the continuing realities of the oppressive function schools serve. Such educational reform efforts concerned with, for example, individual "resilience," are grounded on lies of equal opportunity and mobility, and they individualize the systemic nature of how schools further the interests of power. This should not be read as an attack on public schools (although it is a call for rejecting the plethora of educational research that simultaneously affirms and effaces the oppressive function of schools), but rather as a call for honesty about what schools really do as the first step for planning the remaking of schools into places where democratic cultures flourish and students can learn to imagine human possibilities beyond the market. But, again, building democratic cultures in schools is not enough.

The task for teachers and others committed to the public nature of public schooling is to rethink what democratic schooling could look like to be reimagined in ways that do not subsume what goes on inside schools to relations of capital and other intertwined social relations of domination. What is necessary is for critics of corporatization to make these broad connections between school, society, culture, and power.

These connections involve not only the phenomenon of privatization but also the aforementioned ideology of corporate culture that models schools on corporations. For example, Sara Freedman[17] illustrates how teachers are pressed to write grants while simultaneously the system undermines their capacities to do so. What is more, she demonstrates how making teachers into grant seekers is part of a broader privatization movement that assumes that good "money getting" equals good teaching while denying the extent to which grant-seeking success is tied to cultural capital. Shortly before his death, Bourdieu discussed the way the doctrine of neoliberalism shifts power from what he called the left hand of the state to its right hand. His metaphor meant that part of neoliberal ideology involves undermining investment in the care-giving dimensions of the state historically associated with femininity and shifting these resources to the fiscal and punitive roles of the state historically associated with masculinity. Bourdieu wisely suggests that in this sense neoliberalism is a central issue for feminism to address.[18] Freedman's excellent work addresses this phenomenon in the context of schooling by discussing the merging of the entrepreneurial teacher as grant seeker with the gendered notion of the caring public servant. In addition to the intertwined class and gender dimension of teachers as grant seekers, she also discusses well the racial dynamics.

> [G]rantseeking sanctifies and celebrates a hierarchy within teaching which neatly mirrors the power structure within society at large, all under the guise of insuring more effective teaching to students of color. In the name of educational equity, a competitive process which limits access to vital funds that would support educational equity has been put into place. Grantseeking also works to reinforce a belief in meritocracy and the importance of rewarding the "best and the brightest."[19]

By remaining focused on pedagogical methods, the threat of an abstract notion of "quality education," and pretending that if commercialism can be fended off it will allow students the benefits of a neutral education, some critics of school commercialism miss the extent to which the entire school curriculum is wrapped up with both material and symbolic power struggles or cultural politics — that is, the struggle over values and meanings. One of the central and best aspects of the public nature of public schooling is that in its best forms it allows for the interrogation and questioning of values and beliefs. While historically and currently too much of public schooling has followed an authoritarian model that discourages intellectual curiosity, debate, and a culture of questioning, what makes public schools special is their capacity, by virtue of their public nature, to be places where such a culture of political and ethical questioning can flourish and be developed. The same cannot be said of private for-profit schools. Disney's Celebration School in its corporate community in Celebration, Florida, despite its progressive pedagogical methods, is not likely to encourage questioning about what part ABC Disney plays in the media monopoly. There are, of course, countless examples of public schools that do demonstrate democratic culture.

EDUCATION FOR CRITICAL DEMOCRACY

What is at stake in the battles being waged over Edison Schools and other privatization initiatives in education concerns more than what methods of educational delivery are most effective as both conservatives and liberals are arguing. What is at stake is the role that public schools can play in working to realize a vital and substantive democracy that expands the role of citizens in self-governance concerning issues of economic and resource distribution as well as what and whose cultures, perspectives, and knowledge are valued. From this vantage point, the danger posed by Edison concerns the many ways that Edison threatens to undermine the development of students as critical democratic individuals. This subversion is accomplished in a number of ways.

Whereas education for critical democracy encourages students to be intellectually curious and understand the historical and global dimensions of knowledge, Edison's and other corporate educational programs encourage instrumental approaches to knowledge that emphasize the acquisition of discrete skills and quantifiably measurable performances. Education for critical democracy raises questions about broader structures of power in relation to particular interpretations of truth. Edison and other corporate educational programs disconnect knowledge from the structures of power that inform its creation. Education for critical democracy encourages students to develop the intellectual tools to act to transform the world around them in ways that make a more just and democratic society for everyone. Edison and other corporate models encourage students to think about skills for their exchange value in an economy under the control of others. Education for critical democracy enhances students' capacities to imagine a future in which present inequalities and injustices are overcome and in which history is not inevitable and predetermined but, rather, open to transformation through collective action. Edison and other corporate educational programs teach students that they had better learn to fit in to the present order of things. Education for critical democracy makes hope a social and political project. Edison and other corporate educational programs make hope an individual project expressed through social Darwinism's ideals of survival of the fittest. Education for critical democracy makes individual freedom an ideal fulfilled through helping others to be free. Edison and other corporate educational programs make freedom something you buy at the mall after selling your time to the highest bidder.

How can progressive educators and those committed to schooling for democracy confront these reversals in public and private, the amassing of economic and political power, the threats posed to individuals' capacity to reflect and act on the situation, and the crisis of democracy that involves the undermining of the very possibility of thinking the notion of the public? Those committed to democratic education need to do the following:

1. Understand that the privatization movement is not only about economic and political privatization but the near eradication of notions of the public from public culture, in particular through the production of a culture of cynicism about the possibility for public participation, individual agency, and the possibility of imagining and working for social change;

2. Comprehend how the culture of cynicism that undermines collective public action is pushed by the right and yet unwittingly promoted by liberals and progressives who all too often fail to grasp how central politics is to schooling, pedagogy, and education broadly conceived;

3. Demonstrate that culture, in relation to economy and politics, matters more than ever in addressing the political context;

4. Recognize how pedagogy is central to the project to strengthen and expand a progressive vision of democracy. The project of critical pedagogy informed by cultural studies, critical sociology, mass communications, and feminism is crucial for offering new theories and public vocabularies, to comprehend the relations between public and private spheres and most importantly to focus on the multiple manifestations of neoliberal ideology as they are deployed in multiple sites of knowledge production such as schooling, mass media, and academia. Neoliberal ideology is the most prominent and threatening political movement to any kind of substantive democracy.

The aforementioned constructed culture of cynicism cannot be understood apart from the successes of neoliberalism in making market-based pleasures, hopes, and possibilities the only ones imaginable. As Giroux writes:

The growing lack of justice in American society rises propor-
tionately to the lack of political imagination and collective hope.
We live at a time when the forces and advocates of neoliberalism not only undermine all attempts to revive the culture of
politics as an ethical response to the demise of democratic
public life, but also aggressively wage a war against the very
possibility of creating non-commodified public spheres and
forums that provide the conditions for critical education, link
learning to social change, political agency to the defense of
public goods, and intellectual courage to the refusal to surren-
der knowledge to the highest bidder.[20]

Part of what educators need to do is get beyond the common
sense of the death of politics, the common sense that keeps what
Margaret Thatcher called the TINA thesis intact (There Is No Alternative to the market), the commonsense language that disallows
questioning the relationships between knowledge and authority,
pedagogy, culture, and politics, between theory and transformative
practice, among other relations that are central to democracy as a
process of social self-questioning and ongoing reconstitution.

Although the task ahead for educators, activists, and citizens
more generally may seem daunting, it is important to recognize
the influential work that has been accomplished by opponents
of Edison and other public school privatizers. Groups such as
ACORN (Association of Community Organizations for Reform
Now), Research for Action, PASA (Parents Advocating School
Accountability), CERU (Commercialism in Education Research
Unit), MBEAW (Monterrey Bay Educators Against War), TSJ
(Teachers for Social Justice), to name just a few, have organized
teach-ins, walk-outs, public information events, influenced
school boards, and educated other parents, teachers, and students
about the implications of for-profit schooling as well as the above-
mentioned destructive new education reforms typified by No Child
Left Behind. As teachers, administrators, parents, and students

challenge Edison and other public school profiteers, it is essential for them to understand how Edison is a symptom of a much bigger problem that touches on nearly everything in American life and much around the globe. The same neoliberal ideology that aims to privatize and commercialize schools, to teach students to make an enterprise of themselves, is the same neoliberal ideology that has dismantled welfare and gutted and privatized social services domestically, is the same neoliberal ideology that uses state resources to invest in disciplinary tactics throughout civil society, and is the same neoliberal ideology that the government exports through the threats of military and economic revenge. Recognizing these connections makes these unsettling realities apparent to educators and others concerned about the role of schooling in and for democracy. Challenges to Edison and public school privatization more generally must go beyond criticisms based in effective delivery of instruction measured by test scores. It must begin to address the dangers posed to the promise of a democratic society of the unchecked expansion of corporate power and the infiltration of public schools as a crucial place for the development of a more genuinely democratic society.

NOTES

INTRODUCTION

1 By highlighting Edison's replacement of a national pledge with a corporate one I am not waxing nostalgic for the mandatory uncritical patriotism present in many public schools. Struggles in schools over the symbols of the nation and the meaning of the pledge and patriotism have been discussed brilliantly by Donaldo Macedo, *Literacies of Power* (New York: Westview, 1994) and Henry A. Giroux, *Abandoned Generation: Democracy Beyond the Culture of Fear* (New York: Palgrave/Macmillan, 2003).

2 Alex Molnar, Glen Wilson, and Daniel Allen, "Profiles of For-Profit Education Management Companies: Fifth Annual Report" (Tempe, AZ: Commericalism in Education Research Unit at Arizona State University, January 2003). Available online at www.schoolcommercialism.org.

3 Martha Woodrall, "Edison's Troubles Pile Up," *Philadelphia Inquirer,* May 17, 2002. Jacques Steinberg and Diana B. Henriques, "Market Place; Edison Schools Gets Reprieve: $40 Million in Financing," *The New York Times*, June 5, 2002, p. C1. William C. Symonds, "Edison: An 'F' in Finance," *Business Week*, 3806:2 (November 4, 2002,) 5. Brian O'Reilly and Julia Boorstin, "Why Edison Doesn't Work," *Fortune*, 146:12 (December 9, 2002), 148.

4 According to Edison, fifty-five percent of students are African American and seventeen percent are Hispanic. See Chuck Sudetic, "Reading, Writing, and Revenue," *Mother Jones* (May/June 2001).

5 As of March 22, 2004 a LexisNexis search on Edison Schools contains 613 newspaper articles on "Edison Schools," 442 newspaper
   articles on "Edison Project," and 171 on "Chris Whittle." The vast
   majority concerns the financial viability and "performance" of the
   company. A business news search on Edison Schools for all dates
   contains 806 articles.

6 Michael Dolny, "Spectrum Narrows Further in 2002," *Extra!*
   (July/August 2003).

7 See the important work of Robert W. McChesney, Edward Herman,
   Noam Chomsky, Douglas Kellner, David Corn, and Norman
   Solomon among others on how ownership and profit-seeking affect
   the content of media in a number of ways — in this case to constrict
   the range of possible views.

8 See International Education Indicators published by the National
   Center for Education Statistics. Available online at <nces.ed.gov/
   surveys/international/IntLLndicators/index.asp?SectionNumber=3
   &IndicatorNumber=26>. In reality, the bulk of these incredibly "high
   achieving" schools deprive their privileged students of knowledge
   and skills to understand and criticize the world to move beyond the
   hermetically sealed worldview of the enclaves of privilege.

9 Ibid.

10 For excellent exposés of displaced rage in the city of Buffalo, New
   York, see Julia Hall, *Canal Town Youth* (Albany, NY: SUNY Press,
   2001). See also Pepi Leistyna, *Presence of Mind: Education and the
   Politics of Deception* (New York: Westview, 1999) and his chapter
   "Voices From the Front," *Education as Enforcement,* edited by Ken-
   neth J. Saltman and David Gabbard (New York: Routledge, 2003).

11 PASA. Press Release, "How Voucher Campaign Machinery, Other
   Outsiders Orchestrated Edison 'Parents' Crusade" September 17,
   2001. Available online at <www. pasaorg.tripod.com/edison/pdfs/
   parents.pdf>.

12 Julian Guthrie, "Edison Schools Accused of Discrimination in S.F."
   San Francisco Chronicle, March 27, 2001, p. A11. PASA, "Many African
   American Students Excluded From Edison Test Scores," July 10,
   2001. Available online at www.pasa.org.

13 Ibid.

14 Gary Miron and Brooks Applegate, "An Evaluation of Student Achievement in Edison Schools Opened in 1995 and 1996," The Evaluation Center at Western Michigan University, December 2000. Available online at <http://www.wmich.edu/evalctr/pubs/ecpub.htm>.

15 For an overview of the early experiments in performance contracting, see Carol Ascher, Norm Fruchter, and Robert Berne, *Hard Lessons: Public Schools and Privatization* (New York: Twentieth Century Fund, 1997).

16 Molnar et al., op cit.

17 Knight-Ridder Tribune Business News, "No Agreement Yet on School-Reform Takeover of Philadelphia Schools, *Philadelphia Inquirer*, Friday, November 30, 2001.

18 Carolyn Said, "Balance Sheet Doesn't Back up Edison's Grand Boasts," *San Francisco Chronicle*, July 9, 2002, p. A13. "Edison Schools, Whittle Accused in Suit of Misleading Investors," Bloomberg News, May 15, 2002. Woodrall, op cit.Diana Henriques and Jacques Steinberg, "Edison Schools in Settlement with SEC," *New York Times*, May 15, 2002, p. C1. Symonds, op cit., p. 52. O'Reilly and Boorstin, op cit., p. 148,.

19 Helen Huntley, "Legislators, Teachers Balk at Deal for Edison Schools," *St. Petersburg Times*, September 26, 2003, p. 1E. "National Education Association Warns Florida Retirement System About Risky Investment in Edison Schools," U.S. Newswire, September 30, 2003. Editorial, "Edison Schools Buyout Links Florida to a Loser" *Palm Beach Post*, October 9, 2003, p. 22A.

1 THE RISE AND FALL

1 Vance H. Trimble, *An Empire Undone: The Wild Rise and Hard Fall of Chris Whittle* (New York: Carol Publishing Group, 1995).

2 N. R. Kleinfield, "In Search of the Next Medium," *New York Times*, March 19, 1989, sec. 3, p. 1, col. 2.

3 Ibid.

4 Ibid.

5 Ibid.

6 Ibid.

7 Trimble, op cit.

8 Kleinfield, op cit., p. 1.

9   Trimble, op cit. p. 274.

10 Charles Trueheart, "Chris Whittle's New Thought of School; Is the Edison Project Simple Elitism, or the Future of Education, or Both?" *Washington Post,* July 21, 1992, p. B1.

11 N. R. Kleinfield, "What Is Chris Whittle Teaching Our Children?" *New York Times,* May 19, 1991, sec. 6, p. 32, col. 1.

12 Ibid.

13 Schools for Sale (2003) video produced by Media Education Foundation, featuring Alvin Poussaint, Alex Molnar, and Henry Giroux.

14 Reg Weaver, National Education Association, Press Release, January 22, 2004.

15 Justin Martin, "Lifelong Learning Spells Earnings," *Fortune* 6 (July 1998), 197–200.

16 Trueheart, op cit., p. B1.

17 Trimble, op cit., pp. 8–9.

18 Ibid.

19 Philadelphians United to Support Public Schools, "Community Angered Over Edison Schools' Proposal, Calling It Child Labor," Press Release October 11, 2002. Contact: Aldustus Jordan: 215-563-5848, x12, Helen Gym: 215-808-1400.

20 Trimble, op cit., p. 261.

21 Ibid., p. 266.

22 Ibid., p. 267.

23 Ibid.

24 Ibid.

25 Maryon Allen, "Maryon Allen's Washington," *Washington Post,* June 29, 1980, p. G9.

26 Trimble, op cit., p. 8.

27 Editorial and Comment, "New Ideas; Whittle Project May Provide School Model," *The Columbus Dispatch,* June 2, 1992, 6A.

28 Trimble, op cit., p. 9.

29 About.com, "The Inventions of Thomas Edison." Available online at <http://inventors.about.com/library/inventors/bledison.htm>.

30 Stanley Aronowitz, *How Class Works* (New Haven, Conn.: Yale University Press, 2003).

31 For an excellent criticism of Chubb and Moe, see Jeffrey R. Henig, *Rethinking School Choice* (Princeton, N.J.: Princeton University Press, 1994). See also Kenneth J. Saltman, *Collateral Damage: Corporatizing Public Schools — A Threat to Democracy* (Lanham, Md.: Rowman & Littlefield, 2000).

32 John Chubb, "The System," in *A Primer on America's Schools*, ed. Terry Moe (Stanford, Calif.: Hoover Institution Press, 2001), p. 40.

33 One of the underlying false assumptions of Chubb and Moe's position that the market mechanisms are neutral and apolitical forces. Capitalism, however, is not merely an economic system. It is also a political system in that it organizes hierarchical social relations among people. As Bowles and Gintis put it, "Capitalism, more than a system of resource allocation and income distribution, is a system of governance" (p. xi). This begs the question of why "the rights of ownership should prevail over the rights of democratic citizenry" in determining who is to manage public and private institutions. Samuel Bowles and Herbert Gintis, *Democracy & Capitalism: Property, Community, and the Contradictions of Modern Social Thought* (New York: Basic Books, 1987).

34 On the racial and gendered dimensions of neoliberal rhetoric as it applies to the school reform debates, see Michael Apple, *Educating the Right Way* (New York: Routledge, 2001) and Saltman, op cit.

35 Trimble, op cit.

36 Stuart Elliot, "The Media Business; Whittle Communication's Fall Is Dissected," *New York Times*, October 24, 1994, sec. D, p. 10, col. 4.

37 Ibid.

38 Ibid.

39 Ibid.

40 Ibid.

41 Trimble, op cit., p. 329.

42 Elliot, op cit., p. 10.

43 Ibid.

44 Ibid.

45 Ibid.

46 Peter Applebome, "Entrepreneur Gets $30 Million to Establish For-Profit Schools," *New York Times*, March 17, 1995, p. A20.

47 Edison Timeline from the Education Policy Studies Laboratory at Arizona State University. Available with sources online at http://www.uwm.edu/Dept/CERAI/documents/archives/99/edison.html.

48 Diana Henriques and Jacques Steinberg, "Edison Schools in Settlement with SEC," *New York Times*, May 15, 2002, p. C1.

49 William C. Symonds, "Edison: An 'F' in Finance," *Business Week*, 3806 (November 4, 2002), 52;. Brian O'Reilly and Julia Boorstin, "Why Edison Doesn't Work," *Fortune*, 146:12 (December 9, 2002),

148;. Christopher Byron, "Opinion: Hopelessly Dependent Upon the Generosity of Others," MSNBC (May 16, 2002). Available online at <http://www.msnbc.com/news/753355.asp>.

50 Personal communication. An extensive series of articles and press releases collected and produced by Grannan and her organization PASA can be found on the organization's Web site: pasa.org.

51 Symonds, op cit., p. 52; O'Reilly and Boorstin, op cit., p 148.

52 Jacques Steinberg, "Privatizing Schools," New York Times, April 21, 2002, sec. 4, p. 2, col. 1.

53 Diana B. Henriques, "A Learning Curve for Whittle Venture," New York Times, May 25, 2002, p. C1, col. 4.

54 In order for the argument for economies of scale to make sense it is necessary to assume that authoritative government action could not reduce costs through wide-scale provision of resources the way it does in many government departments. In other words, for the argument of economies of scale to make sense one first must think of schooling as a business rather than a public good.

55 Mensah M. Dean, "Reformers Standing by Edison/Will Wait out Firm's Financial Troubles," Philadelphia Daily News, May 16, 2002.

56 Parents Advocating School Accountability, "Concerning Possible Edison Saviour's Controversial Ultra-Right History." Available online at http://pasaorg.tripod.com/edison/edison.html. The quote appears in Ryan Lizza, "Silent Partner," New Republic, 222:2 (January 10, 2000).

57 Ibid. See also <http://www.opensecrets.org/newsletter/ce72/06 thirdparties.asp>.

58 <http://www.publiceye.org/research/Group_Watch/Entries-131.htm>. Elton Manzione, "The Private Spy Agency," National Reporter (Summer 1985). (Incidentally, the story of the no longer published National Reporter is a fascinating one of student dissent worthy of its own book.)

59 Byron, op cit.

60 Jacques Steinberg, "Philadelphians Jittery Over Plan to Privatize 20 Schools," New York Times, May 20, 2002.

61 Jacques Steinberg and Diana B. Henriques, "Market Place; Edison Schools Gets Reprieve: $40 Million in Financing," New York Times, June 5, 2002, p. C1.

62 Carolyn Said, "Balance Sheet Doesn't Back up Edison's Grand Boasts," San Francisco Chronicle, July 9, 2002, p. A13.

63 Business/Financial Desk, "Edison Schools Get $40 Million in Loans," *New York Times*, June 5, 2002, p. A1.

64 Alex Molnar, Glen Wilson, and Daniel Allen, "Profiles of For-Profit Education Management Companies: Fifth Annual Report" (Tempe, AZ: Commericalism in Education Research Unit at Arizona State University, January 2003), p. 5. Available online at www.school-commercialism.org.

65 "Edison Schools, Whittle Accused in Suit of Misleading Investors," Bloomberg News, May 15, 2002.

66 Martha Woodrall, "Edison's Troubles Pile Up," *Philadelphia Inquirer,* May 17, 2002.

67 F. Howard Nelson, "Trends in Student Achievement for Edison Schools, Inc.: The Emerging Track Record." Available online at www.aft.org, p.8; Gary Miron and Brooks Applegate, "An Evaluation of Student Achievement in Edison Schools Opened in 1995 and 1996," The Evaluation Center at Western Michigan University, p. xxviii. Available online at www.wmich.edu/evalctr; Patrick Groff, "Success For All: Research and Reform in Elementary Education," *Teachers College Record* 105:1 (2003); B. Greenlee and D. Bruner, "Effects of Success for All Reading Program on Reading Achievement in Title 1 Schools," *Education 122* (2001), 77–188; Stanley Pogrow, "The Unsubstantiated 'Success' of Success for All: Implications for Policy, Practice, and the Soul of Our Profession,". *Phi Delta Kappan 81* (2000), 596–600; S. M. Ross and L. Smith, "Effects of the Success for All Model on Kindergarten through Second-Grade Reading Achievement, Teachers' Adjustment, and Classroom Climate at an Inner-City School," *Elementary School Journal 95* (1994), 121–38; L. Smith, S. M. Ross, and J. Casey, "Multi-Site Comparison of the Effects of Success for All on Reading Achievement," *Journal of Literacy Research 28,* (1996), 329–53; H. J. Walberg and R. C. Greenberg, "The Diogenes Factor," *Phi Delta Kappan 81* (1999), 127–28; H. J. Walberg and R.C. Greenberg, "Educators Should Require Evidence." *Phi Delta Kappan 81* (1999), 132–35; Stanley Pogrow, "Success for All Is a Failure," *Phi Delta Kappan* (February 2002).

68 Dan Primack, "Leeds Weld Reverses Course" BuyOuts (September 8, 2003).

69 Ibid.

70 Ibid.

71 Ibid.

72 Helen Huntley, "Legislators, Teachers Balk at Deal for Edison Schools," *St. Petersburg Times*, September 26, 2003, p. 1E.

73 Bloomberg News, "Edison Schools CEO Gets $344,999 Pay Raise," *Newsday*, August 26, 2003, p. A50

74 Huntley, op cit., p. E1.

75 Ibid.

76 Ibid.

77 Ibid.

78 "National Education Association Warns Florida Retirement System About Risky Investment in Edison Schools" U.S. Newswire, September 30, 2003.

79 Ibid.

80 Les Kjos, "Analysis: Pension Fund Seeks Edison" United Press International, October 6, 2003.

81 Editorial, "Edison Schools Buyout Links Florida to a Loser," *Palm Beach Post*, October 9, 2003, p. 22A.

82 Ibid.

83 Available online at www.tallahassee.com/mid/democrat/news/opinion/6974527.htm.

84 "Edison Investment Is Risky Business for Retirees, Say Groups; Gov. Bush's Staff Knew Florida Money Manager Used Unsound Practices" U.S. Newswire, November 12, 2003.

2 BUT DOES IT WORK?

1 A number of writers have recently responded critically to the standardization and standards movement from a number of different perspectives, ranging from the philosophical to the practical: Howard Gardner, Deborah Meiers, Peter Sacks, Alfie Kohn, and Stephen Jay Gould, authors associated with The Rethinking Schools collective, are just a few.

2 Diana Jean Schemo, "Charter Schools Trail in Results, U.S. Data Reveals" New York Times, Front page August 17, 2004. See also how the administration responded in Diana Jean Schemo, "U.S. Cutting Back on Details in Data About Charter Schools" August 29, 2004.

3 Gary Miron and Brooks Applegate, "An Evaluation of Student Achievement in Edison Schools Opened in 1995 and 1996" The Evaluation Center at Western Michigan University, p. xxviii. Available online at www.wmich.edu/evalctr.

4 Quoted in the PBS *Frontline* Web site for the TV documentary "Public Schools, Inc." Available online at www.pbs.org/wgbh/pages/frontline/shows/edison/etc/links.html.

5 Ibid.

6 Ibid.

7 F. Howard Nelson, "Trends in Student Achievement for Edison Schools, Inc.: The Emerging Track Record." Available online at www.aft.org, p.8.

8 PBS *Frontline* Web site, op cit.

9 Ibid.

10 Caroline Grannan, "Low Performance at More Schools Further Discredits Company's 'Gains' Boast," Press Release, Parents Advocating School Accountability, November 18, 2001. Available online at <http://pasaorg.tripod.com/edison/pdfs/postivell.pdf>.

11 Josh Funk, "Teachers: Edison Was Warned," *Wichita Eagle*, February 3, 2002.

12 Ibid.

13 Ibid.

14 Editorial, *Wichita Eagle*, February 5, 2002.

15 N. R. Kleinfield, "For-Profit Grade Schols Planned," *New York Times*, May 15, 1991, p. A25, col. 1.

16 Laurel Shaper Walters, "Schmidt Leaves Yale for School Experiment," *Christian Science Monitor*, May 28, 1992, p. 7.

17 Charles Trueheart, "Chris Whittle's New Thought of School; Is the Edison Project Simple Elitism, or the Future of Education, or Both?" *Washington Post*, July 21, 1992, p. B1.

18 Alex Molnar, *Giving Kids the Business* (New York: HarperCollins, 1998), p. 75

19 Social critic bell hooks has made this point well in many of her numerous books.

20 Excellent sources of information on the racial and ethnic dimensions of poverty and income inequality can be obtained at www.census.gov and from the Bureau of Labor Statistics at www.bls.gov, as well as in James Heintz and Nancy Folbre, *The Ultimate Field Guide to the U.S. Economy: A Compact and Irreverent Guide to Economic Life in America* (New York: The New Press, 2000). See also www.inequality.org and www.livingwagecampaign.org.

21 Pierre Bourdieu and Jean-Claude Passeron, *Reproduction: In Education, Society, and Culture*, trans. R. Nice (Beverly Hills, Calif.: Sage, 1977).

22 Raymond Williams, *The Long Revolution* (Peterborough, Ontario: Broadview Press, 2001), p. 67.

23 Miron and Applegate, op cit., p. xxviii.

24 Jacques Steinberg, "Buying in to the Company School," *New York Times,* February 17, 2002.

25 Joan Walsh, "The Shame of San Francisco," Salon.com, March 29, 2001. Available at <http://dir.salon.com/news/feature/2001/03/29/edison/index.html?sid=1021431>.

26 Patrick Groff, "Success For All: Research and Reform in Elementary Education," *Teachers College Record,* 105:1 (2003). Available online at www.tcrecord.org. Groff includes the following references, quoted here verbatim: Greenlee, B. & Bruner, D. (2001). "Effects of Success for All reading program on reading achievement in Title 1 schools." *Education, 122,* 177–188; Pogrow, S. (2000). "The unsubstantiated 'success' of Success for All: Implications for policy, practice, and the soul of our profession." *Phi Delta Kappan, 81,* 596–600; Ross, S. M., & Smith, L. (1994). "Effects of the Success for All model on kindergarten through second-grade reading achievement, teachers' adjustment, and classroom climate at an inner-city school." *Elementary School Journal, 95,* 121–138; Smith, L., Ross, S. M., & Casey J. (1996). "Multi-site comparison of the effects of Success for All on reading achievement." *Journal of Literacy Research, 28,* 329–353; Walberg, H. J. & Greenberg, R. C. (1999). "The Diogenes factor." *Phi Delta Kappan, 81,* 127–128; Walberg, H. J. & Greenberg, R. C. (1999). "Educators should require evidence." *Phi Delta Kappan, 81,* 132–135.

27 Ibid.

28 Stanley Pogrow, "Success for All Is a Failure" *Phi Delta Kappan* (February 2002).

29 Available online at http://www.naschools.org/contentViewer.asp?highlightID=7&catID=40.

30 Available online at http://www.naschools.org/news/newsviewer.asp?highlightID=20&docID=714.

31 Alfie Kohn, "Introduction: The 500-Pound Gorilla" in *Education, Inc.,* by Alfie Kohn and Patrick Shannon (Portsmouth, N.H.: Heinemann, 2002), pp. 7–8.

32 Ibid., p. 8.

33 Henry Giroux, *Teachers as Intellectuals: Toward a Critical Pedagogy of Learning* (Westport, Conn.: Greenwood Publishing Group, 1994).

34 John Dewey, *Reconstruction in Philosophy* (New York: Beacon, 1990).

35 Steven A. Jacobson, *Central Yup'ik and the Schools: A Handbook for Teachers*, 3rd ed. (Juneau: Alaska Native Language Center, 1998). Available online at http://www.alaskool.org/language/central_yupik/yupik.html.

36 A. Fienup-Riordan, *Eskimo Essays* (New Brunswick, N.J.: Rutgers University Press, 1990).

37 McDowell Group, *Alaska Native and American Indian Education: A Review of the Literature* (Juneau: First Alaskans Foundation, 2001). Available online at: http://www.ankn.uaf.edu/summit/McDowell/reviewhistory.html.

38 An exceptionally egregious example of this is Abigail and Stephen Thernstrom, *No Excuses: Closing the Racial Gap in Learning* (New York: Simon & Shuster, 2003) that, in the tradition of racist sociology, blames African American culture for the legacies of educational and economic racial exclusion. For a brilliant review of this tradition in the field of sociology, see Robin D. G. Kelley, *Yo Mama's Dysfunktional!* (New York: Beacon, 1997). *No Excuses* was funded by the rightwing Olin Foundation and Earhart Foundation, which matters in part because the book blames public schooling for allowing African Americans to be hurt by their pathological culture and concludes that weakening teachers' unions and privatizing public schools are the solution to "helping" African Americans with the problem that is their culture.

39 Available online as a link to the Kent, Washington implementation Web site at <http://www.kent.k12.wa.us/curriculum/math/edmath/gr5/unit4.html>. Also available online at http://mathforum.org/paths/fractions/mars.hunt.html as posted by the Math Forum of Drexel University.

40 Consumers Union/Parents Television Council quoted at www.mediareform.net/media/tenthings.php.

41 Despite the potential for serving the public interest, public television and radio is frequently a mouthpiece for both the state and private sector. Public interest and state control are not synonymous. State institutions are sites of struggle for democratic versus statist and corporatist control. See the important mass media work of Robert W. McChesney, such as *Rich Media, Poor Democracy* (New York: The New Press, 2000).

42 James Heintz and Nancy Folbre, *The Ultimate Field Guide to the U.S. Economy: A Compact and Irreverent Guide to Economic Life in America* (New York: The New Press, 2000).

43 Childhood Poverty Research Brief 2, "Child Poverty in the States: Levels and Trends From 1979 to 1998." Available online at www.nccp. org.

44 Henry A. Giroux, *The Abandoned Generation: Democracy Beyond the Culture of Fear* (New York: Palgrave/Macmillan, 2003), pp. xviii–xix.

45 Editorial, "CEOs: Why They're So Unloved," *Business Week* (April 22, 2002).

3 EDRON: TWO BRIEF STUDIES IN CORPORATE UNACCOUNTABILITY

1 Rene Sanchez, "For-Profit Public Schools Show Hope After First Year," *Washington Post*, December 10, 1996, p. A1.

2 Jordana Hart, "Charter Schools Get Nod to Open," *Boston Globe*, December 10, 1994.

3 Ibid.

4 Jon Marcus, "Going Private — the US experience," *The Independent* (London), June 18, 1998, p. 7.

5 Ibid.

6 Sanchez, op cit., p. A1.

7 Ibid.

8 Ibid.

9 Editorial, "Extra Credit for Renaissance," *Boston Globe*, February 13, 1997, p. A24.

10 Ibid.

11 Marcus, op cit., p. 7.

12 Ibid.

13 Ibid.

14 Muriel Cohen, "Roger Harris Eager for Challenge of Renaissance Job," *Boston Globe*, May 31, 1998, City Weekly, p. 1.

15 Ibid.

16 Ibid.

17 Ibid.

18 Ibid.

19 Ibid.

20 Rebecca Winters, "USA: Trouble for Schools Inc." Time.com, May 27, 2002. Available online at <www.corpwatch.org>.

21 Peggy Farber, "Boston: Renaissance Charter School," *The American Prospect*, 9:39 (July 1, 1998–August 1, 1998).

22 Ibid.

23 Editorial, "A Lesson in Education," *Boston Globe*, August 20, 2002, p. A18.

24 Staff, "Big Charter School in Boston Breaks Its Ties With Edison," *New York Times*, May 17, 2002, p. A21.

25 Daniel Golden, "Boston School Severs Its Ties with Edison, Citing Test Scores," *Wall Street Journal*, May 16, 2002.

26 Staff, op cit., p. A21.

27 Ibid.

28 Tanya Schevitz, Nanette Asimov, and Chronicle Staff Writers, "Edison School Vote Could Be Invalid," *San Francisco Chronicle*, June 25, 1998, p. A14.

29 Ken Romines, "Edison School Revisited," *San Francisco Chronicle*, June 10, 1999, p. A25.

30 Ibid.

31 Nanette Asimov, "For-Profit Edison Avoids Teacher Walk-Out, Agrees to Raise Salaries," *San Francisco Chronicle*, June 16, 2000, San Francisco Friday, p. 3.

32 Philadelphians United to Support Public Schools, "Community Angered Over Edison Schools' Proposal, Calling It Child Labor," Press Release, October 11, 2002. Contact: Aldustus Jordan: 215-563-5848, x12, Helen Gym: 215-808-1400. Available online at <http://pasaorg.tripod.com/edison/edison.html>.

33 Jay Mathews, "Putting For-Profit Company to the Test," *Washington Post*, April 30, 2002, p. A9.

34 Asimov, op cit., p. 3.

35 Nanette Asimov, "Few S.F. Schools Make Target Test Scores," *San Francisco Chronicle*, October 5, 2000, p. A17.

36 There is a large body of literature on this subject by such scholars as Samuel Bowles, Herbert Gintis, Jean Anyon, Jeannie Oakes, Paul Willis. An excellent recent discussion of it can be found in Ellen Brantlinger, *Dividing Classes: How the Middle Class Negotiates and Rationalizes School Advantage* (New York: RoutledgeFalmer, 2003).

37 Debra J. Saunders, "Edison Is Ground Zero in Education Battle," *San Francisco Chronicle*, January 28, 2001, p. B11.

38 Ibid. (Saunders also bizarrely red-baited Wynns and Sanchez intimating that their anticorporate stance on public schooling was communist, which she defines as "an even distribution of ignorance," and then writes that Wynns and Sanchez are ironically pushing for "capitalism," which she defines as "more money for teachers.")

39 Dana Woldow, Editorial Letter "Edison School Fuss," *San Francisco Chronicle*, February 2, 2001.

40 PASA, "Many African American Students Excluded From Edison Test Scores," July 10, 2001. Available online at www.pasa.org.

41 San Francisco Unified School District test score data. Available online at http://orb.sfusd.k12.ca.us/schdata.htm.

42 Nanette Asimov, "Soft Money Pours Into Schools Race," *San Francisco Chronicle*, November 4, 2000, p. A17.

43 Ibid.

44 Ibid.

45 Ibid.

46 Julian Guthrie, "S.F. Poised to Cancel Edison Charter," *San Francisco Chronicle*, February 10, 2001, p. A15.

47 Julian Guthrie, "Edison Schools Accused of Discrimination in S.F.," *San Francisco Chronicle*, March 27, 2001, A11.

48 Ibid.

49 Ibid.

50 Julian Guthrie, "S.F. Schools Vote to End Edison Compact," *San Francisco Chronicle*, June 29, 2001, A1.

51 Ibid.

52 Ibid.

53 Ibid.

54 Mathews, op cit., p. A9.

55 Stephanie Salter, "For-Profit Edison Still in the Red," *San Francisco Chronicle*, June 9, 2002, p. D4.

56 Mathews, op cit., p. A9.

57 Karen Breslau and Nadine Joseph, "Education: Edison's Report Card," *Newsweek* (July 2, 2001), 48.

4 NO CONTEST: EDISON'S TAKEOVER OF THE PHILADELPHIA SCHOOLS AND THE LESSONS OF PUBLIC SCHOOL COMPETITION

1 Stephen Phillips, "Edison Cast Out of Flagship," *Times Educational Supplement*, May 24, 2002, International, p. 18

2 Knight-Ridder Tribune Business News, "No Agreement Yet on School-Reform Takeover of Philadelphia Schools," *Philadelphia Inquirer*, November 30, 2001.

3 Ibid.

4 Editorial, "Philly Outflanks N.Y.C. on Schools," *Daily News*, August 13, 2001, p. 34.

5 Michael A. Fletcher, "Philadelphia's Schools to Be Privately Run Under Pa. Plan," *Washington Post*, November 6, 2001, p. A1.

6 Ibid.

7 Brent Staples, "Editorial Observer; A Case of Radical Surgery on Failing Schools," *New York Times*, June 10, 2001, sec. 4, p. 14.

8 Dale Mezzacappa, "Hundreds Protest Takeover of Philadelphia Schools," *Philadelphia Inquirer*, November 29, 2001.

9 Ibid.

10 Jacques Steinberg, "Fight in Philadelphia Over Schools Takeover," *New York Times*, November 15, 2001.

11 Jacques Steinberg, "Pennsylvania Abandons Plan to Privatize School Offices," *New York Times*, November 21, 2001, p. A14.

12 Ibid.

13 Ibid.

14 Ibid.

15 Jacques Steinberg, "Private Groups Get 42 Schools in Philadelphia," *New York Times*, April 18, 2002, p. A1.

16 William C. Symonds, "Edison: An 'F' in Finance," *Business Week*, 3806 (November 4, 2002) 52.

17 For an excellent account of the Chicago reforms and their relationship to local, national, and global configurations of economic and political power, see Pauline Lipman, *High Stakes Education: Inequality, Globalization, and Urban School Reform* (New York: Routledge/Falmer, 2004).

18 Brian O'Reilly and Julia Boorstin, "Why Edison Doesn't Work," *Fortune* 146:12 (December 9, 2002), 148.

19 Catherine Gewertz, *Education Week*, 22:13 (November 27, 2002), 3.

20 Ibid.

21 Ibid.

22 Mary Lord, "Philly's Fresh Start," *U.S. News & World Report*, 133:13 (October 7, 2002), 52.

23 Symonds, op cit., p. 52.

24 O'Reilly and Boorstin, op cit., p. 148.

25 Ibid.

26 John O'Neil, "Who Profits When For-Profits Run Schools?" *NEA Today*, 21:1 (September 2002), p. 31.

27 Ibid.

28 David B. Caruso, "School Privatization Firms Asked to Take Less Pay," Associated Press, May 23, 2003.

29 Ibid.

30 Ibid.

31 Eric Tucker, "Vallas Drops Plan to Cut Per-Pupil Funding for Firms Running Troubled Schools," Associated Press, May 31, 2003.

32 Ibid.

33 Ibid.

34 David B. Caruso, "Museums, Hospitals and Colleges May Join Philadelphia's Experiment in School Privatization," Associated Press, June 16, 2003.

35 David B. Caruso, "Colleges Lend Aid to Philadelphia School Reform Effort," Associated Press, August 12, 2003.

36 Ibid.

37 Two useful reports on K12 are Gerald Bracey, "Knowledge Universe and Virtual Schools: Educational Breakthrough or Digital Raid on the Public Treasury?" Education Policy Studies Laboratory, April 2004. Available online at http://www.asu.edu/educ/epsl/EPRU/documents/EPSL-0404-118-EPRU.doc ; Susan Ohanian, "The K12 Virtual Primary School History Curriculum," Education Policy Studies Laboratory, April 2004. Available online at http://www.asu.edu/educ/epsl/EPRU/documents/EPSL-0404-117-EPRU.doc.

38 Steinberg, "Pennsylvania Abandons Plan," op cit., p. A14.

39 For excellent and extensive coverage of the relationship between ownership and content of corporate media, see Robert W. McChesney, *Rich Media, Poor Democracy* (New York: The New Press, 1999). See also Robert W. McChesney and David Corn, *Our Media Not Theirs* (New York: Seven Stories Press, 2003).

40 Peg Tyre, Barbara Kantrowitz, Suzanne Smalley, and Pat Wingert, "Philly's Tough Lessons," *Newsweek*, 140:17 (October 21, 2002), 60.

41 Brent Staples, "Editorial Observer; A Case of Radical Surgery on Failing Schools," *New York Times*, June 10, 2001, sec. 4, p. 14.

42 "About a fifth of African Americans and Latinos work at the low end of the occupational ladder, in poorly paid service jobs. Not surprisingly, they are underrepresented in managerial and professional occupations. Only 21% of African Americans and 15% of Latinos held such jobs in 1998 compared with 31% of white workers." James Heintz, Nancy Folbre, and the Center for Popular Economics, *The Ultimate Field Guide to the U.S. Economy* (New York: The New Press, 2000), p. 75. "In 1995 women held less than 9 percent of corporate-

officer positions in Fortune 500 companies, according to Catalyst, a New York-based organization that promotes the interests of women in business. Last year they held close to 16 percent.... Of those 2,140 women, 163 were black — a minuscule proportion." Ellis Cose and Allison Samuels, "The Black Gender Gap" *Newsweek*, 141:9 (March 3, 2003), 46.

43 Heintz et al., op cit., p. 76.

44 Fletcher, op cit., p. A1.

45 Stephen Metcalf, "Reading Between the Lines," *The Nation*, January 28, 2002. Reprinted in Alfie Kohn and Patrick Shannon, eds., *Education, Inc.* (New York: Heinemann, 2002), p. 51.

46 For important insights on what the new testing really accomplishes see for example, Stan Karp, "Bush Plan Fails Schools," *Rethinking Schools*, 15:3 (Spring 2001). See also Bertell Ollman, "Lesson Plans: Why So Many Exams?" *Z Magazine*, 15:11 (October 2002); Pierre Bourdieu and Jean Claude Passeron, *Reproduction in Education, Society, and Culture* (London: Sage, 1990).

47 Henry A. Giroux, "Leaving Most Children Behind," in *Abandoned Generation: Democracy Beyond the Culture of Fear* (New York: Palgrave/Macmillan, 2003), chap. 4; Stan Karp, "The No Child Left Behind Hoax." Available online at < http://www.rethinking-schools.org/special_reports/bushplan/hoax.shtml>.

48 See, for example, Carol Ascher, Norm Fruchter, and Robert Berne, *Hard Lessons: Public Schools and Privatization* (New York: Twentieth Century Fund, 1997), which gives an excellent history of the failure of early privatization experiments.

5 CORPORATE SCHOOLING AND THE FUTURE OF THE PUBLIC

1 Robert W. McChesney, introduction to *Profit Over People,* by Noam Chomsky (New York: Seven Stories Press, 1999), p. 7.

2 As Noam Chomsky points out in *Profits Over People* (New York: Seven Stories, 1999), those who espouse neoliberal ideology do not apply their own supposed free market ideals to challenge the current transfers of public wealth to private interests in the form of tax credits, direct payment, corporate welfare, and the public support of entire industries such as defense and agriculture.

3 Mark Zepezauer and Arthur Naiman, *Take the Rich Off Welfare* (Tucson, AZ: Odonian Press, 1996).

4 Bill Moyers, "This is Your Story — The Progressive Story of America. Pass It On," text of speech to the Take Back America Conference sponsored by the Campaign for America's Future, June 4, 2003.

5 Pierre Bourdieu and Loic Wacquant discuss this in the excellent film, *Sociology as a Martial Art* (2001). In the U.S. context, see Robin Truth Goodman, *World, Class, Women* (New York: Routledge, 2003).

6 Henry Giroux, *The Abandoned Generation: Democracy Beyond the Culture of Fear* (New York: Palgrave/Macmillan, 2003).

7 David Welna, Morning Edition, National Public Radio, April 8, 2002.

8 For brilliant and extended discussion of what is wrong with the New War on Terror, see Noam Chomsky *9-11* (New York: Seven Stories, 2001) as well as the many insightful articles available online on Z-net www.lbbs.org. In the context of education, see Kenneth J. Saltman and David A. Gabbard (eds.), *Education as Enforcement: The Militarization and Corporatization of Schools*, (New York: Routledge, 2003).

9 A few of the higher-profile yet hardly unique cases are Colombia, the occupied Palestinian territories, Afghanistan, Iraq, etc. Currently, the U.S. military has a presence in about 140 countries and is a top weapons dealer yet fails miserably in comparison with Europe when it comes to genuinely humanitarian aid.

10 See Ziauddin Sardar and Merryl Wyn Davies, *Why Do People Hate America?* (New York: Disinformation Company, 2002) for an excellent history of how U.S. foreign policy has created animosity against the United States around the world. In the context of schooling, see Saltman and Gabbard, op cit.

11 Racial profiling against predominantly African Americans has been given a great lease on life, as September 11 has been used to justify the racial profiling of Muslim Americans. According to the American Civil Liberties Union, the Bush Administration's ban on racial profiling announced in June 2003 is symbolic but does not provide for enforcement. For an excellent discussion of the threat to civil liberties posed by the U.S. Patriot Act, see Nancy Chang, *Silencing Political Dissent: How Post-September 11 Anti-Terrorism Measures Threaten Our Civil Liberties* (New York: Seven Stories Press, 2002).

12 See, for example, David Harvey, *The New Imperialism* (Oxford: Oxford University Press, 2003).

13 Ellen Meiskins Wood, "Kosovo and the New Imperialism", in Tariq Ali (ed.) *Masters of the Universe?: NATO's Balkan Crusade* (New York: Verso, 2000), pp. 190–202; Ellen Meiskins Wood, *Empire of Capital* (New York: Verso, 2003).

14 Jeffrey Henig, *Rethinking School Choice* for a history of the racist origins of voucher schemes.

15 Makani N. Themba, "Choice" and Other White Lies," in *Education, Inc.*, edited by Alfie Kohn and Patrick Shannon (New York: Heinemann, 2002), pp. 143–44.

16 Alfie Kohn and Patrick Shannon (eds.) *Education, Inc.* (New York: Heinemann, 2002).

17 Sara Freedman, "Teachers as Grantseekers," *Teachers College Record*, 102:2 (2000), 398–441.

18 Boudieu discusses this and Loic Waquant comments on it in the film, *Sociology as a Martial Art*, op cit. On neoliberalism, critical education, and gender, see Robin Truth Goodman, *World, Class, Women* (Routledge: New York, 2003).

19 Freedman, op cit., p. 432.

20 Henry Giroux, *Public Spaces, Private Lives: Beyond the Culture of Cynicism* (Lanham, MD: Rowman & Littlefield, 2001), p. xii.

INDEX